Indonesian
Cross-Gender Dancer
DIDIK NINI THOWOK

Osaka University Press

Osaka University West Front,
2-7 Yamadaoka, Suita-shi,
Osaka, Japan 565-0871

Published in Japan
by Osaka University Press
First published 2018
—

Indonesian Cross-Gender Dancer
DIDIK NINI THOWOK
Auther: MADOKA FUKUOKA
Photographer: HITOSHI FURUYA
English version copyright
© MADOKA FUKUOKA

Design: Shirai Design Studio
YOSHIHISA SHIRAI, TAKUMI EGAWA
—

Original Japanese edition
published by Mekong Publishing
Company, Tokyo
© 2014, text by MADOKA FUKUOKA
pictures by HITOSHI FURUYA

All rights reserved.
No part of this publication may be
reproduced or transmitted in
any form or by any means,
electronic or mechanical,
including photocopy, recording,
or information storage and retrieval
systems, without permission in
writing from the publisher.

ISBN 978-4-87259-598-7

▶ The scene of battle
dance from the work
Dwimuka Hip-Hop,
as a modern retelling.
Didik created this work
in 2012.

Didik acts as Ardhanareesvara.
2013 in Candi Pelaosan Temple.
To express the androgynous figure of
Hindu god, Didik puts the makeup
and wears the costume of asymmetrical
colors, also he wears original
asymmetrical mask on his back.

Didik performs the Chinese dance with long ribbon. It is one of the scenes of the work *Panca Sari*. 2013 in Parangkusumo.

The variation on a scene from the work *Panca Sari*. 2013 in Parangkusumo.

The variation on the final scene of the work *Panca Sari*. 2013 in Parangkusumo.

The performance of "anger". It is the final scene of the work *Dewi Sarak Jodag*. After her original form is revealed, Sarak Jodag expresses anger and devilishness because of the shame she feels. The deep red color of the mask symbolizes human desire and violence in Java. This is the original mask that inspired by *Hannya* mask in Japanese *noh* theater. Didik expresses the emotion of the woman who is out of self-control using the dance movements of the demon king's character in the Javanese masked dance.

Indonesian Cross-Gender Dancer Didik Nini Thowok

Madoka Fukuoka

Photographer:
Hitoshi Furuya

Osaka University Press

Acknowledgements

This book is the translation of my Japanese book entitled *Sei wo koeru dancer* (The dancer who transcends the gender boundary). The book was published by Mekong Publishing Company in Tokyo, Japan in May, 2014. After the publication of the Japanese version, my photographer friend, Hitoshi Furuya and I, had several discussions on preparing an English version. Didik Nini Thowok saw his 60th birthday on November 2014 and held the special event entitled "REBORN" in Yogyakarta at the end of that year. The event consisted of several performances and a seminar on cross-gender performances. We attended all the performances and the seminar at the event and it was an opportunity for us to appreciate again his energy and maturity as an artist, as well as an entertainer and organizer. Although the contents of this English version are almost the same as the Japanese version, we have added some new descriptions and audio visual materials.

We would like to thank Mas Didik Nini Thowok, his family, and the staff members in his dance studio for all their support and cooperation. (Terima kasih banyak atas semua bantuan dari Mas Didik, keluarganya dan para staff di studio.)

This publication was supported by JSPS KAKENHI Grant Number 16HP6003 of Grant- in Aid for Publication of Scientific Research Results. Osaka University Press supported the editing of this book. Especially I received much support and advice from Nobuyo Kawakami and Shiori Bando in the process of writing this book.

I would like to thank my friend, Ibu Marjorie Suanda, who translated the interview section of this book from the Indonesian language to English.

Also I would like to thank my English teacher, Mrs Marian Dohma, who supported proofreading the texts of this book.

Finally, I would like to thank my family, especially my husband, Shota, and our two daughters, Ayu and Saya, for their support during the production of this book.

15th June 2017   MADOKA FUKUOKA

Contents

- Introduction — 017
  - Column 1 Yogyakarta, an Old City in Central Java — 022

1 Crossing the Boundary of Gender:
Female-Impersonation in Traditional Dance — 023
1-1 Female-Impersonation in Javanese Dance — 024
1-2 Femininity and Masculinity — 027
1-3 The Body of a Female-Impersonating Dancer — 028
1-4 Traditional Dance in Java and Bali — 029

2 In Search of Multiple Identities:
Creative Work *Dwimuka* — 039
2-1 *Dwimuka* Dance — 041
  Highlights in the Work *Dwimuka* — 042
2-2 *Dwimuka Jepindo* — 042
  Column 2 The Mask Dance of Cirebon, Java — 046

3 Crossing the Boundary of Ethnic Identity:
Creative Work *Panca Sari* — 051
3-1 As an Artist of Chinese Indonesian Descent — 052
  Column 3 People of Chinese Descent in
  Suharto-Governed Indonesia — 056
3-2 In Search of Identity — 056
  Highlights of *Panca Sari* — 062

4 From Comedy to Serious Performance:
The Creative Work *Dewi Sarak Jodag* — 063
4-1 Comedian — 064
4-2 Encountering Japanese *Onnagata* (Female-Role Players) — 066
4-3 Serious Work *Dewi Sarak Jodag* — 068
  Highlights of *Dewi Sarak Jodag* — 069
  Column 4 Javanese Panji Romance — 072

5 As an Indonesian Dancer — 073

5-1	As a Chinese Indonesian Artist	074
5-2	Network of Chinese Descendant Communities	075
5-3	The Chinese Temple in Gudo, East Java	076
5-4	Chinese New Year in Yogyakarta	081

6 The Body of a Female-Impersonating Dancer — 085

6-1	Training the Body	086
6-2	Devices for Transformation by Masks:	
	Multiple Expressions of Gender	091

7 From the Local Community to the World — 095

7-1	Teachers	096
7-2	An Artist in a Local Place	096
7-3	Performances in Various Regions of the World	099

8 As a Manager of a Studio, as a Teacher — 105

8-1	Education of Staff	106
8-2	Composition of Works	110
8-3	The Next Generation	115

9 The 2014 Event REBORN — 117

• Afterword — 125

| | Afterword: MADOKA FUKUOKA | 126 |
| | Afterword: HITOSHI FURUYA | 131 |

• Appendix DVD — 135

DVD Contents 1
Dance Works of DIDIK NINI THOWOK	137
DVD Contents 2 Street Walk Yogyakarta	137
DVD Contents 3 Interview by MADOKA FUKUOKA	
(Translation by MARJORIE SUANDA)	138
• Bibliography	150
• Index	152

Introduction

Introduction

Didik Nini Thowok is an Indonesian female-impersonating dancer originally from Java island.

 Indonesia, the largest island country in Southeast Asia, is known for its abundant natural resources and growing economy. Also, the various genres of performing arts of this country attract many people from around the world. Didik is actively involved in the creative industry in Yogyakarta, Java island. Yogyakarta, the center of a royal culture that attracts many tourists, and an area for experimental artistic creation, is now a focal point for both traditional art forms and innovative artistic endeavors. Among the various kinds of well-known traditional performing art forms in this region, are *gamelan*, a large ensemble of metal instruments, *wayang*, a form of shadow puppet theater, *topeng*, a masked dance, and *sendratari* or dance theater. Abundant genres of folk performing-art

©HITOSHI FURUYA, Tokyo, 2004: A performance of *Golek Lambangsari*, a traditional Javanese dance, in Yogyakarta style

forms, such as the folk theater, *ketoprak*, and the horse dance *jatilan (kuda kepang)*, can also be seen there.

In Yogyakarta, a center of tradition as well as a center of the creative arts, Didik Nini Thowok is famous for his original creative activities, which are based on the revitalization of traditional dances. There are a variety of traditions of transgender performances and dance forms in Javanese theater. Whereas the tradition of male impersonation by female performers can still be seen, such as in performances for tourists, the tradition of female impersonation by male dancers is rare today. In this situation, Didik is a dancer who has revitalized the tradition of this type of transgender performance.

Didik was born in 1954 in Tumanggung, Central Java, to a Chinese father and a Javanese mother. His father operated a leather workshop during Didik's childhood. Didik entered the National Dance Academy in 1974 and for eight years learned traditional Javanese dancing as well as various other kinds of Indonesian dances (Janarto 2005: 77). After his graduation, he focused on the management of his dance studio named "Natya Lakshita". From then, he has been engaged in artistic activities and the education of dancers of the next generation.

In the 1960s, Indonesians of Chinese descent began to experience many difficulties in Indonesia because of the government's so-called assimilation policy, and for a long time, severe restrictions were placed on their cultural expressions. Since the resignation of Suharto, who ruled the country with an iron fist for 32 years (1966–1998), the so-called assimilation policies have been gradually relaxed. However, there are many artists who suffered from this assimilation policy during their most active years, and Didik, as an artist of Chinese descent, also experienced restrictions on his artistic expressions.

His unique artistic activities which cross the gender boundary also reflect the problems associated with his ethnic identity as a Chinese Indonesian. Under the conditions that made it difficult to directly express his own ethnic identity, he produced many works that deconstruct the stereotypes of both gender and ethnicity. However, Didik does not directly criticise these stereotypes. Rather, he presents various kinds of expressions of gender and ethnicity, attracting audiences with his trained body, excellent skills, and original and singular ideas.

The strength of Didik's performances lies in his expression of various aspects of femininity with his trained body and excellent skills. His body makes possible expressions of all features of female behavior, such as elegant beauty, delicate movement, dynamic power, comical pitifulness, and violent devilishness. How can he achieve these multiple expressions? They arise from his talent, his slender body, and from the skills and spiritual power of traditional Javanese dance that he studied for a long time, his exploration of and respect for various kinds of Asian dances, his dedicated endeavors and his daily training.

As both an artist and a human being, his career path and his thoughts have a great affect on his artistic activities. He makes us aware of multiple feminine qualities and various kinds of ethnicities, and of differences in humanity. He shows his charm when he performs as an actor on stage with his own particular aura. He is a theatrical genius who can read an atmosphere and immediately perform the kind of material the audience wishes to see.

He is a unique dancer and many people from around the world have traveled to see him. In his career he transcends the boundaries of gender and ethnicity. By presenting his representative works, I will consider his development toward accomplishing female impersonation[1].

---

1 I had my first opportunity to see Didik perform in 2004. Although his works
  have been observed by a number of researchers since the 1990s,
  I am mostly familiar with his activities from 2004 to the time of writing.

© Didik Nini Thowok Entertainment:
Didik Nini Thowok wearing a Javanese male costume

Column 1
Yogyakarta, an Old City in Central Java

Yogyakarta, known as a historical location, is the center of Indonesia's court culture. This city, where traditional art forms have been handed on, boasts tourism sights that attract people from all over the world. There are various kinds of performing art forms staged for tourists in this city. In the royal palace, people can enjoy periodical performances of music and dancing. In the Sonobudoyo museum, which is close to the palace, people can see shadow puppet plays every night. The dramatic dance performances of the epic poem "Ramayana", named *sendratari* Ramayana can be seen at the open air theater at the famous historical location of Prambanan and also in the open air theater at the center of the city's Prawisata.

The current sultan is Hamengkubuwono X. He also holds the position of the governor of the special region of Yogyakarta, which has a sister relationship with Kyoto prefecture in Japan, and so he has visited Japan many times often accompanied by groups of performing artists as a goodwill gesture. From the high quality of their performances, we can see that Yogyakarta is a place where various kinds of traditional cultures have been nurtured.

Many unique dancers have also come from this city. The National Art Institute (ISI Yogyakarta) which consists of departments of music, dance, theater, fine arts, etc. is a center for education of various kinds of art forms. The predecessor of this institute was the National Dance Academy (ASTI Yogyakarta), founded in 1963. At the department of dance, students learn various kinds of Indonesian dance as well as Javanese dance in the Yogyakarta style. Additionally, they learn the art of creating dance works.

We can also see many attempts at creating dance works outside of the Institute. There are many private dance studios managed by dancers, and some studios encourage the creation of dance works. The representative one is the studio of Bagong Kussudiardjo (1928–2004) where Didik also had become a disciple. Even today, many dancers manage private studios.

In Yogyakarta, the historical accumulation of traditional art forms is evident along with the atmosphere of flexibility towards adopting new elements.

▲ © Madoka Fukuoka, Yogyakarta, 2012: *Srimpi* dance in Yogyakarta court
▼ © Madoka Fukuoka, Yogyakarta, 2012: Klana *topeng* in Yogyakarta court

© Madoka Fukuoka, Yogyakarta, 2012: A shadow puppet or *wayang kulit* performance in Sonobudoyo Museum in Yogyakarta

I

Crossing the Boundary of Gender: Female-Impersonation in Traditional Dance

1-1
Female-Impersonation in Javanese Dance

The existence of transgender actors or dancers is recognized in Javanese performing art forms. In this tradition, there are two cases, where male dancers perform female roles, and where female dancers perform male roles. Presently, all students of the National Art Institute's department of dance learn the basis both of male and female dances. Outside the Institute, female dancers or actresses performing male roles can still be seen, but there are few performances where male dancers perform female roles.

As James Peacock wrote in his monumental work, there were female-role dancers and singers in East Javanese folk theater, *ludruk*. He described the transvestite dancers and singers as a symbolic of "refined" appearances and acting (Peacock 1987: 52–53, 168–172).

Peacock's description informs us of the special position held by Javanese female-role dancers or actors in the past. For the court dance *bedhaya* in Yogyakarta, there was a tradition where boys performed dances as females. Also, in the Banyumas district, in southern central Java, the *lengger* dance, where female-role dancers appear, can still be seen. Through Didik's study of various kinds of dances in Java, he has experienced the tradition of female-role play and recognizes its uniqueness.

▲ ▶ © Didik Nini Thowok Entertainment: A performance of the *lengger* dance of Banyumas, a play featuring Dariah (86 years old), a female-impersonating dancer from Banyumas

2 There are several types of characters in Javanese dance such as "refined male", "nimble male", "rough male", "refined female", "nimble female" etc.
The representative character of "refined male" is, for example, the role of prince Rama in the epic poem Ramayana.

Didik has an innate expertise in dressing up as a woman and performing female dances. Through his learning experience at the National Dance Academy, Didik felt that he was best suited to the role of a "refined male character"[2]. The physical movements of a "refined male character" are similar to those of female dancers, thus making the transition to a female role relatively easy (Janarto 2005: 65–69). In addition, Didik often performed female dances during his childhood, as seen in a photograph of him performing for his high school classmates. Didik became seriously interested in creating female dance works during the late 1970s, and produced several female dance performances for students at his dance studio. After these works were performed at an Indonesian dance contest and they received excellent reviews, he was encouraged to establish his career as a cross-gender dancer.

Also, he desired to revitalize the tradition of playing female roles, which was disappearing. To realize his ideal, he has continued his endeavor to revitalize the tradition of female-role playing, through his original ideas and stage directions.

Besides the acting of female-roles in traditional performing art forms, there are also transvestite males known as *banci* or *waria* in Indonesia[3]. Strictly speaking, they are in a different category from the performers of traditional art performances; however, there are some common points,

[3] Boellstorff pointed out that most *waria* see themselves as men who (1) have the souls of women from birth, (2) dress as women much of the time, (3) have sex with "normal" men (Boellstorff 2003: 231). However, the third point is not always true especially in Java. There are *warias* who do not have sexual relationships with men. Rather, the second point is more characteristic. Boellstorff also emphasized the transvestite power of *waria* to change the public appearances of others (Boellstorff 2003: 22). Thus the *waria* is the category where the cultural skills are important.

025   1 Crossing the Boundary of Gender: Female-Impersonation in Traditional Dance

such as the skills in cross dressing and the acting of female roles, and also in their daily professions, such as dancers, singers, and beauticians (Oetomo 1996: 262).

In 2006, there was heated controversy about the "Anti Pornography and Pornoaction Bill" (*Undang-Undang Anti Pornografi dan Pornoaksi*, known as the acronym UU APP) in Indonesia (Lindsay 2011: 183)[4]. The supporters of the enforcement of this bill, as well as some Islamist organizations, considered traditional dance costumes that expose the arms or shoulders, and dance performances that have erotic elements, as symbols of backward values and they criticized them. In the court tradition in Yogyakarta, the various kinds of performing arts that have originated since the Hindu-Java period can be found. Many of the dancers' costumes exposed the shoulders and arms, as is the case with the traditional wedding costumes in the royal court. Many disputes have occurred about this bill. Whether these dances and costumes are a tradition that should be protected or a custom that should be revised and whether "traditions" or "customs" should be included as elements in the discussion is under consideration.

Many artists and researchers opposed the bill. Didik has also opposed the view that traditional dances and costumes can be considered to be pornography.

He insists on the necessity for careful consideration of the boundary between pornography and custom or tradition. The bill, if totally passed, would have a great affect on the continuance of the traditional Javanese dances. This applies even more so to female-impersonating dancers, as many critics of them are concerned about their transgender expressions, and transvestite links and status. Didik has participated in a demonstration and in a Javanese organization for sexual minorities.

There are conflicts between the continuance of traditions and customs and modern and religious values. In this complicated situation, Didik has continued his artistic activities while wishing to revitalize the Javanese dance tradition with new, original elements.

---

[4] Jennifer Lindsay described the debate as follows: When the text of this draft became public in early 2006, debate erupted as people realized the drafting process had been hijacked by Islamic parties and groups, and that the proposed bill was no longer a matter of media regulation of pornography (for which there was wide community support), but an attempt to use the pornography issue to implement sharia-influenced law to control public morality, dress and behavior (Lindsay 2011:183). The issue of the costumes of traditional dancing was also included in this debate.

I-2
Femininity and Masculinity

What kind of femininity can be seen in his performances? In the cases where he performs classical female dances, he explores "traditional femininity" in all aspects such as costumes, makeup, hairstyles, and physical movement. Such typical "femininity" of traditional dancing includes appearance, refined acting and movement, and deft physique.

Then, what is the ideal femininity for Javanese classical dance?

We can see elegant and modest female characters in shadow puppet theaters and dance dramas, many of which derived from a story-world based on ancient Indian epic poems. These stereotypical femininities are in opposition to typical ideal masculinities, where mental aptitude, physical strength, and victory in battle are important elements [5].

To realize the traditional idea of femininity, Didik has learnt how to assume an elegant frame and perform gentle physical movements as well as how to apply makeup to enhance feminine aspects in his appearance. On the other hand, he also explores different kinds of femininities, which he achieves by mastering various kinds of dancing where quick and dynamic movements are important.

© MADOKA FUKUOKA: Prince Rama and Princess Sita in a dance drama from Ramayana

[5] Examples of typical female "refined characters" include Princess Sita in the epic Ramayana, and Subadra in the epic Mahabharata. Examples of typical male ones include the husbands of each of them, Prince Rama and Arjuna.

I-3
The Body of a Female-Impersonating Dancer

In appearance, Didik is a tall, slender man with a refined disposition. As well as delicacy, his body also has litheness and strength. In his original works, Didik performs the comicality of an unsophisticated old woman, or emotions of anger as well as the beauty of a refined woman.

After mastering central Javanese traditional dances in the National Dance Academy, he also studied Western and Eastern Javanese dances and Balinese dances. Based on the central Javanese style that he originally mastered, he has

© NAOYA IKEGAMI: Practice of a Japanese traditional dance

studied many traditional dance styles in various regions of Indonesia. In the process of studying these female dances, he has always explored high-level skills and trained his body to be that of an ideal female-impersonating dancer. Up to the present day, almost all of his original works have been female-impersonating dances, and he is one of the few artists to have consistently performed as a female-impersonating dancer.

He has also studied abroad, such as in Japan, India, and China. While a number of Indonesian dance creators were influenced by concepts of Western art, Didik not only mastered dances from Indonesia, Japan, India and China but also combined these dance forms in his creations. This mastering of various traditional arts had become a rich source of his expression of female-impersonation. However, such acquisition of knowledge has not limited him to using it as a behind-the-scenes inspiration for his new creations. He is also a highly professional on-stage performer of each traditional dance form (Mrázek 2005: 253, 271). In regard to the Japanese style, he stayed in Japan from 1999 to 2000 as a fellow of the Japan Foundation, and studied Japanese traditional dance and the dances of the *noh* theater. The experiences resulted in the 2001 performance of *Bedhaya Hagoromo* (Hughes-Freeland 2008: 7–20)[6].

1-4
Traditional Dance in Java and Bali

Traditional Javanese dancing is characterized by smooth movements that are often compared to flowing water. The dancers of classical Javanese dance step slowly, as they shift their weight. Didik, as a dancer who originated from central Java, is a master and elegant dancer of female dance genres from the classical Javanese repertoire.

Golek Lambangsari dance. *Golek* refers to a rod puppet, and *Lambangsari* is the title of a piece of music. *Golek* dance is known as an elegant female dance that partly derived from the movement of rod puppets. This dance features

---

[6] Hughes-Freeland considered this work from various viewpoints (Hughes-Freeland 2010; 2012). She described its creative process, particularly with regard to interweaving established practice (tradition) and invention or innovation (Hughes-Freeland 2010: 42–43) as well as the framework of "hybridity" in this work (Hughes-Freeland 2012).

the young girl's gestures of making up and grooming. We can see the close resemblance between the structure of rod puppets and the movements of the human dancers. The body of a Javanese rod puppet consists of joints at the neck, shoulders, arms, and wrists. This body structure is conveyed in the human dancers' movements, as the choreography features movements of the upper part of the body, such as the arms and neck. In traditional Javanese dancing we can see the elegant and beautiful arm, hand, and neck movements, and also the sophisticated line of sight as downcast eyes are incorporated.

Gambyong Pangkur. This dance derived from the welcome dance or the dance of the meeting of young males and females. *Pangkur* is the title of a piece of music. The costume that covers the upper part of the dancer's body is a winding fabric named *kemben*. This costume exposes the dancer's shoulders and arms, and reveals the movements of the upper part of the body. Elegant and subtle movements that imitate grooming and putting on makeup are also the

© HITOSHI FURUYA, Tokyo, 2004:
A traditional dance of Yogyakarta, Java: *Golek Lambangsari*

characteristics of this dance.

Balinese *legong* dance: This is one of Didik's specialties. This dance features the quick movements of a young girl. Balinese *legong* contains quick movements and sudden changes of rhythm that contrast with the classical Javanese dancing that is compared to flowing water. Both litheness and dynamics can be seen in the dance movement.

Being attracted by the energy of dance in Bali, where Hindu rituals and culture are deeply rooted, Didik learned *legong* dance from a Balinese master, I Gusti Gede Raka, over a long period. Didik often uses elements of Balinese dancing in his original creative dance works. His performance is of such high standard that he is the popular dancer in Bali, and has participated in a performance tour of Balinese dancers that traveled to Europe.

Jaipongan is a popular folk dance from West Java. This dance was created between the late 1970s and early 1980s, and is based on the West Javanese folk dance, *ketuk tilu*, and a martial art dance named *penca silat*. The accompanying

drum rhythm, which features original percussion sounds, slows and quickens the music, and dynamic dance movements are the characteristics of *jaipongan*.

Beskalan Putri is a female dance from East Java, depicting the appearance of general femininity. Didik learned this dance from a maestro of East Javanese female role dancing, Rasimun, being a disciple of Rasimun for a long time in order to master this original dancing. The most characteristic element of this performance is the handling of the original costume. The dancer wears a black velvet costume with gold embroidery and places a large stole around his shoulders, which he handles during the performance. Also, the dancer wears bells around his ankles and incorporates the sounds that these make in the performance. Didik's tall stature looks particularly striking in this performance.

Didik is a dancer who can differentiate between the various kinds of dances from various regions. For the performance of Javanese and Balinese dances, the dancer exposes much of his upper body, with movements that are also important, such as those of the neck, shoulders, arms, and hands and fingers. Not only is he a talented dancer, but Didik also has the tall and slender body that is suitable for female-impersonating performances. He achieves both smooth movements and dynamic, quick movements.

© HITOSHI FURUYA, Tokyo, 2004:
A performance of a Javanese *Gambyong* dance

© Didik Nini Thowok Entertainment: A *jaipongan* dance from West Java

1 Crossing the Boundary of Gender: Female-Impersonation in Traditional Dance

© Hitoshi Furuya, Yokohama, 2009:
The Balinese traditional dance
Legong Bapan Saba

© Hitoshi Furuya, Tokyo, 2004:
Beskalan Putri from East Java

© Hitoshi Furuya, Tokyo, 2004: *Beskalan Putri* from East Java

2

In Search of
Multiple Identities:
Creative Work
Dwimuka

In addition to the ideal femininities in the traditional dances, Didik has also explored the expressions of other dimensions of femininity such as an ugly woman, an old woman, a comical woman, and the roughness of women. He often says that he wants to express women as human beings and depict not only their beauty but also their many other dimensions[7].

To realize this, he often observes people on the street and then mimics them. His acute observations of humanity allow him to realize expressions that transcend the audience's expectations. Gaining an insight into the true nature of women, he can deviate from the stereotypes of women.

In his creative works, he expresses the ugliness or fearfulness of women using comical masks and movements, and brings the audience to laughter. As a master of unorthodox expressions, Didik deviates from ideal stereotypical versions of femininity and presents conflicting elements of femininity.

© Didik Nini Thowok Entertainment:
A performance of the *Dwimuka* dance

[7] According to Didik, "By having ugly women appear on stage, I try to show that, in reality, many aspects besides beauty live inside of every woman". This comment explains the multiple facets of females depicted in his performances and reminds us of the comparative equation noted in the Snow White Complex by Elissa Melamed in which beauty=youth=good versus ugliness=old=evil. In the folklore, the comparison between a beautiful young princess and an ugly old woman (or a witch) typically concludes with a "happy ending" for the princess. However, both sides reside in a single woman, and Melamed elucidates that life feels lengthened after youth is lost (cf. Melamed 1983).

Dwimuka Dance

The creative work *Dwimuka* is Didik's specialty. *Dwimuka* means "two faces". Didik's inspiration to wear masks on the front and back of his head came from his watching of horror movies. In this dance, the performance facing backwards is especially demanding, and Didik makes fullest use of his skills to achieve this. Didik frequently receives requests for this dance both in Indonesia and abroad. During the Suharto regime, Didik had received requests from the president and the president's special guests several times. The creative works that are entitled *Dwimuka* consist of seven or more works in total. Some cases involve using five masks, such as the work entitled *Panca Muka*, which means "five faces". In his seven works, he employs the various combinations of masks, such as Japanese and Indonesian, Javanese, and Balinese.

© Hitoshi Furuya, 2013: The *Dwimuka* dance

Highlights in the Work *Dwimuka*

The characteristic element to note in this work is Didik's skill and technique. As well as the costume and mask devices, his skill in performing while facing backwards is such that the audience is not aware that he is facing backwards. This is also the prominent characteristic of this work. His skill in this work is the result of his various types of practice, including practice using a mirror in front and behind him. When he is facing backwards we see the amazing flexibility of his body. His device of changing costume on the stage is derived from the changing costume mask dance of Cirebon, West Java. There are many versions of his *Dwimuka* works. In some works, there are comical scenes featuring an ugly or old woman. There is a variety of mask and of stage directions relating to the expressions on the masks.

2-2

Dwimuka Jepindo

One of the famous works is entitled *Dwimuka Jepindo*. This work incorporates aspects of Javanese and Japanese dance, and its title is a compound word derived from "Jepang" (the Indonesian term for Japanese) and "Indo" (a common abbreviation for Indonesian).

The performance begins with Didik's back towards the audience as he performs a dynamic folk dance in Javanese costume and mask. Accompanied by the rhythm patterns of the drums, this dance is extremely difficult because he must complete the various movements while facing away from the audience.

The music changes in the second scene, and Didik performs a classical Japanese dance while slowly turning to face the audience. At this point, the audience realizes that Didik actually performed the first scene while facing backwards and they applaud the dancer.

Sometimes a Chinese dance with a long ribbon and an Indian *Bharathanatyam* dance are staged in the scene that follows.

When performed in Indonesia, especially in Bali, a Balinese *legong* dance is staged as a third scene. Taking off the mask and wearing an accessorized wig, Didik performs *legong* dance, dancing nimbly. This manner of quickly changing the mask and costume on stage is a characteristic of classical Japanese dance, and also includes an element of the traditional Javanese mask dances of Cirebon in which performers typically change masks or parts of their costumes on stage.

At the conclusion of the third scene, the dancer moves upstage to remove the costume and accessorized wig. He then dons a wig with a Javanese woman's bun, and performs a West Javanese *jaipongan* dance without a mask in the fourth scene. In the fifth scene, Didik wears a mask that depicts an ugly woman and a wig with a shaven hairstyle. The initial appearance alone causes the audience to giggle, but the subsequent comical performance causes outbursts of laughter. In the sixth and final scene, he dons a long cloth,

© HITOSHI FURUYA, 2013: The first scene of *Dwimuka Jepindo*, performing a Javanese dance facing backwards

which covers the head, and a mask of an old woman. While emulating the stiff movements of an elderly person, he then performs a surprisingly aerobic dance routine, which inspires laughter from the audience.

They are surprised by the wide variety of movements his body can perform. And by his use of masks as equipment for transformation, he presents multiple ethnicities and femininities. This is his original method of deconstructing a single ethnicity and femininity [8].

When he performs his creative works, he wears costumes of his own original design. In *Dwimuka Jepindo*, for performing six kinds of scenes, he wears three layers of costumes [9].

To prepare for the performance, he begins by first putting on the costume for the last scene, and the costume for the next scene over that. To create the appearance for the backwards-facing mask, he puts undergarments on the back of his body. After this, he wears an original two-sided dance costume. The front of this costume is a Japanese *kimono* while the back is a Javanese dance costume. To match the costumes, the mask over his face is that of a Japanese woman named "Otafuku" while the one on the back of his head is a mask of a Javanese woman. Appropriately, the

© Hitoshi Furuya, 2013: The first scene of *Dwimuka Jepindo*, performing a Japanese dance wearing an Otafuku mask

---

[8] Mrázek analyzed Didik's works and performances as a reflection of his unique personality and life experiences. He also discussed Didik's identity and conducted an analysis of gender boundaries and ethnic boundaries (Mrázek 2005).

unique wig includes a bun at the front and long black hair at the back. He also wears necklaces hanging from the front and the back of his neck.

Regarding the physical dance movements, *Dwimuka Jepindo* is essentially based on conventional genres of dance which require a high level of skill to perform. The Javanese folk dance in the first scene is characterized by dynamic movements that Didik convincingly performs with his back to the audience. In the classical Japanese dance in the second scene, a comical mask of a Japanese woman is worn and graceful movements are achieved by utilizing the sleeves of the kimono and a fan. The Balinese dance in the third scene accentuates Didik's physique and virtuosic technique as he performs a highly energetic Balinese *legong* dance with a technique comparable to that of a female Balinese dancer. In the fourth scene, he acts as a traditional Javanese dancer which demonstrates his technique in that particular dance form. In the fifth scene, he dons a mask and wig of an ugly woman while performing a comical act, while in the sixth and final scene, he disguises himself as an old woman and brings the audience to laughter by pretending to be breathless during an aerobic dance.

© Hitoshi Furuya, 2013: The first act of *Dwimuka*. performing a Chinese dance facing backwards

9 As for the use of costumes in *Dwimuka Jepindo*, see my article (Fukuoka 2014: 67–74).

Column 2

The Mask Dance of Cirebon, Java

Among the variety of masked dances of Java known as *topeng*, one of the most famous is *topeng* Cirebon, from the Cirebon region on the north coast of Java. Cirebon refers to the city and prefecture of that name, as well as a number of neighboring prefectures. In this region, *topeng* Cirebon is performed in conjunction with circumcision rites, marriage ceremonies, and other occasions marking important life events, as well as with planting, harvesting, and other agricultural rituals.

The performance of *topeng* Cirebon is conducted at the host person's or host village's request and is sponsored by them.

In the performance, held in the daytime in many cases, the solo dancer, who leads a troupe of approximately 15 members, uses five masks and performs the acts with a clown figure. Although the style of dance varies according to each village, at present the dance-centered masked performances now occupy the mainstream. The dancer performs as a stylized character, or *watak*, for each mask, portraying a refined or *linyep* character through a number of stages before arriving at a rough or *gagah* character.

Topeng Cirebon is most often complemented by a shadow puppet play or *wayang kulit*, with the former presented in the daytime and the latter at night. Furthermore, most *topeng* dancers belong to the lineage of the puppeteers of shadow plays, or *dalang*, with some even being puppeteers themselves. Against this background, it is not surprising that *topeng* dancers in Cirebon are called *dalang topeng*.

In the 1970s, Didik studied under the master dancer, Suji, in the Palimanan region. After that he studied under the master dancer, Sawitri, in the Losari region, and under Rasinah in Indramayu prefecture. Although there are many male dancers of *topeng* Cirebon, all these three of Didik's teachers were women. Additionally, all of them are known as dancers who exude a charismatic aura.

Didik also studied the performance of male-impersonation dances from his three female teachers. These experiences had a great affect on his performance of female-impersonation.

© Hitoshi Furuya:
Mask of the Cirebonese mask dance.
Rumyang, owned by Didik Nini Thowok

© Hitoshi Furuya:
Mask of the Cirebonese mask dance.
Klana, owned by Didik Nini Thowok

▶ © Hitoshi Furuya:
A performance of Rasinah.
A mask dance dancer from Indramayu

© Hitoshi Furuya, Taman Sari, 2013: The variation of *Dwimuka*. Clockwise from the center (1) Battle dance of *Dwimuka Hip-Hop*. (2) Balinese *legong* dance from *Dwimuka Jali*. (3) Didik wears the shop-bought mask on his back and performs the beautiful woman from *Dwimuka Hip-Hop*. (4) Didik wears the mask of Panji in Cirebon area on his back. It is a scene of *Dwimuka Festop*. (5) Didik wears the mask of Sarak Jodag on his back. It is a scene of *Dwimuka Jali*.

© Didik Nini Thowok Entertainment (around 1979):
Didik and Suji, a maestro of mask dance in Palimanan

3

Crossing the
Boundary of
Ethnic Identity:
Creative Work
Panca Sari

3-1
As an Artist of Chinese Indonesian Descent

Didik was born in 1954 in Tumanggung, Central Java, the eldest son among five siblings.

His paternal grandparents were from Fujian (Fukien), a southeast part of China. Didik's father had been brought up by his uncle, three of the wives of whom were Javanese. Didik's grandfather had started to run a workshop in the leather industry in 1950, and Didik's father took over that factory. Didik's mother ran a small stall selling daily goods.

As a result of this family structure, Didik grew up being familiar with both Chinese and Javanese culture from an early age. Didik remembers that his Chinese grandfather often listened to Javanese shadow puppet plays or popular theater programs broadcasted by the National Radio station, Yogyakarta Branch.

On the other hand, Didik also had opportunities to experience Chinese culture, such as Chinese puppet plays or lion dances, especially as his father was a talented performer of these. Being busy with the workshop in daily life, Didik's father participated in events for Chinese people on festive days and performed lion dances or dragon dances.

© Didik Nini Thowok Entertainment: Being held by his Chinese grandfather

© Didik Nini Thowok Entertainment: Relatives on his mother's side

10 Didik remembered that he had many opportunities to see Indian films on open air screens in the public squares called "*layar tancap*". In the French film director Mersonne's 2014 film entitled *Garuda Power*, we can know that many screenings by *layar tancap* had be done in Indonesia since around the 1950's.

He is also tall and often took the part of the hind legs of the lion or the tail part of the dragon. Didik had many opportunities to witness his father's dynamic dancing and performances.

Didik has also been influenced by Indian films[10]. The Hindi film star, Raj Kapoor, was a popular idol in Java. Particularly Didik was attracted to the dancing and costumes of Indian films. Also, he was deeply attracted to the plays featuring female-impersonating dancers in Javanese folk theater.

This small town in Central Java fostered an environment for the co-existence of multi-cultural practices until the early 1960s.

However, this environment of multi-cultural co-existence suddenly vanished. In 1965, the political disturbance known as G30S (30th Sep. movement) occurred, and from then the people of Chinese descent living in Indonesia began to experience severe difficulties. Under Suharto, who overthrew Sukarno, Indonesia's first president, the lives of people of Chinese descent came to be restricted in various ways.

Heryanto (2014) described that under Suharto order, access for Chinese Indonesians to state education and public service was limited. Also, Chinese names for persons, organizations, and businesses had to be Indonesianized. The Chinese language, mass media, and organizations were eliminated and prohibited (Heryanto 2014: 140)[11].

© Hitoshi Furuya, Jatimulyo, northwest of Yogyakarta: Didik's parents in front of Didik's home

[11] Heryanto described the circumstances as follows: Culturally, "Chineseness" was declared foreign; politically and morally it was perceived to be detrimental to the Indonesian Self as officially constructed (Heryanto 2014:140).

They were forbidden to display elements of Chinese culture in the public sphere. These restrictions were presented as an "assimilation" policy. However, people of Chinese descent were not included in the ethnic groups of Indonesia, and were subjected to various kinds of prohibitions and discrimination in Indonesian society (Tsuda 2011: 13). Chinese performing arts, which had been popular until the first half of the 1960s, could not be performed after this political change.

Didik was in junior high school at this time. He was the only student of Chinese descent with a Chinese name in his class and suffered severe bullying from his peers. He still vividly remembers being denounced as a "Cina", having stones thrown at him, and being beaten up. These were fearful times for him and deeply affected the boy's mentality. He became introverted, fearful, shy, and afraid to appear in public. It was dancing that supported him. When he performed Javanese or Balinese dances, he could receive applause from the audience. Particularly he obtained self confidence when he performed comedic acts and caused the audience to laugh. On the stage, the boy's

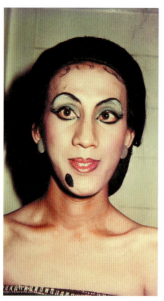

© Didik Nini Thowok Entertainment: A performance of the work "Nini Thowok" (The point was a mole drawn by him)

© HITOSHI FURUYA: The ritual of Nini Thowok, held near Yogyakarta

heart, which had been wounded by racial stigmatization, could find the power of expression. When performing, wearing costumes and makeup, he could regain self confidence. Dancing was his hope and support.

In 1974, he entered the National Dance Academy in Yogyakarta. It was a turning point for him to become a dancer of Javanese dances. Since then, he has developed his career by learning a range of kinds of dancing, including female dances. He has realized his ambition of being a dancer of "refined" character dances.

His stage name, Nini Thowok, was derived from a creative work from his school days in the National Dance Academy[12]. The work was a collaborative one by three dancers in the academy, including Didik. This work, based on a traditional Javanese ritual, involved a doll named Nini Thowok. In this work, Didik acted the role of an old woman performing a ritual, and he was brought into the spotlight. This performance was the turning point for him to become a female-impersonating dancer.

He also received education from dancers outside of the academy. Many of his experiences were from apprenticeships under creative dancers or traditional dancers named "maestros". After finishing his nine years of study in the academy, he graduated in 1983. The various elements of Javanese dances had become part of him, and became the basis of his artistic expression.

After his graduation, he began to teach the art of using stage makeup (*tata rias*) at the National Dance Academy. He also considered the possibility of staying at the academy; however, he experienced how very difficult it was for people of Chinese descent to work in an academy where Javanese art forms were taught. In addition to this, he was receiving increasing numbers of requests from overseas for performances. In 1980, while he was studying at the academy, he had founded his own dance company, Natya Lakshita. After careful consideration, he decided to concentrate on managing this company. Since then, he has been running this company, using modern management methods, handling the education of his students and the performance activities.

---

[12] Dance education at Indonesian art institutions place importance on creativity based on tradition as well as on learning about local, traditional dances. In addition, the influences of Indonesian cultural policies aimed at developing a new national culture based on the cultural traditions of various regions can be seen (Sutton 1991). National Dance Academy in Yogyakarta has been one of the representative centres of creative activities in Indonesia.

Column 3

People of Chinese Descent in Suharto-Governed Indonesia

Under the Suharto government, which lasted for 32 years (from 1966 to 1998), people of Chinese descent were considered to be obstructions to national unity and were under the pressure of so-called "assimilation". Although this "assimilation" was designed to transform them from being Chinese, these people were still categorized as "foreign residents" or *warga keturunan asing*, excluded from many ethnic groups in Indonesia, and were discriminated against (Tsuda 2011:13). An anthropologist, Ariel Heryanto, analyzed this situation of Chinese Indonesians under the Suharto order as "ethnic minority under erasure" (Heryanto 2014:138–144).

As mentioned above, the teaching of Chinese languages, the publishing and importation of Chinese books, and celebrating traditional Chinese events were forbidden under the Suharto regime. Chinese signage disappeared from Chinatown, and any associations that consisted of only individuals of Chinese descent were forbidden. Through these prohibitions, Chinese elements were excluded from language, education, and culture (Aoki 2006: 402). The acquisition of Indonesian nationality was promoted and all people of Chinese descent were obligated to have an Indonesian name.

Since the resignation of Suharto, the circumstances have been changing. Signboards written in Chinese have reappeared in the towns, books written in Chinese have been published, and academic studies about Chinese culture also have been growing. The number of young people of Chinese descent learning the Chinese language has been increasing (Aoki 2006: 411). The events or festivals associated with the Chinese New Year have become popular and Chinese temples (*klenteng*), as the bases for these events, have been obtaining an important position in society (Tsuda 2010).

These changing circumstances can also be seen in the Indonesian film industry. In 2002, a young female director, Nia Dinata, directed a film that focused on the history and existence of Chinese people in Indonesia. Entitled *Ca Bau Kan*, this film is appreciated as a representation of the Chinese people who were ignored for a long period of Indonesian history.

On February 2013, in the city of Yogyakarta, a gate to mark the entrance to the local China town was constructed and Chinese New Year was celebrated enthusiastically. Didik participated in this event as one of the committee members, and he performed a Chinese mask dance at the opening ceremony, and one of his own works, based on the legend of a white snake, at the closing ceremony. The performance of this event demonstrated the change in society and the trend of acceptance of Chinese cultural expressions in public spaces.

3-2

In search of Identity

Under the Suharto-regime (1966–1998), ethnic Chinese people often experienced fear and danger, and many artists of Chinese descent experienced difficulties in expressing their ethnic identity. Didik as a *peranakan* (Chinese

Indonesian) artist, suffered the process of losing half of his ethnic identity. In such social conditions, the artists could not express their true ethnic identities.

Although we can see the elements of Chinese dance and music in Didik's works, we cannot see his clear conscious expression of "Chineseness" in his works, especially until 2010. He had previously concentrated on expressing multiple identities, not drawing direct attention to his Chinese identity.

This is his method of objecting to the prejudicial concept that a person can have only one single identity. Also, it is an indication of his flexibility, accepting multiple cultural traditions from his own family background. Didik has indicated his disagreement with the essentialized prejudice that the artistic expressions of Chinese artists always include "Chineseness". Often adopting Chinese elements in his works, he did not, however, focus on them, as he included them with other ethnic elements. He has always featured various other elements of Indonesian culture. As

© Didik Nini Thowok Entertainment:
The masked dance performing

well as the Chinese elements, we can see the Javanese elements, Balinese elements, Indian elements, Japanese elements and also modern dance, aerobics dance, etc., in his works. In this way he explores and expresses the diversity of Indonesian or Asian culture.

One of his creative works is entitled *Panca Sari*, which means "five elements". In this work, Didik presents Chinese, Western, Javanese and Balinese clowns' elements, and the elements of Indian songs. In the first scene, he performs a Chinese dance accompanied by Chinese music, manipulating a long ribbon. In the second scene, he wears a Javanese mask and shows his skill in Javanese dancing with Javanese folk music. In the third scene, the music changes drastically to one of disco dancing, and he performs a robotic dance as a street dancer and performs the robot dance with a gold-colored shop-bought mask. In the fourth scene, he wears a Balinese clown mask and performs a comical play. Finally, in the last act, he wears a monkey mask and dances with the accompaniment of *dangdut*

▲ ▶ © HITOSHI FURUYA, Gudo, East Java, 2011: Performing a Chinese dance in the first scene of *Panca Sari* in a Chinese temple

© Hitoshi Furuya, Gudo, East Java, 2011: Performing a Javanese female dance in the second scene of *Panca Sari* in a Chinese temple

© Hitoshi Furuya, Gudo, East Java, 2011: Marionette-like dancing with a Balinese mask in the fourth scene of *Panca Sari* in a Chinese temple

© Hitoshi Furuya, Gudo, East Java, 2011: Robot-like dancing in the performance of a street dance in the third scene of *Panca Sari* in a Chinese temple

music, which originated from Indian film music[13]. There are many comical elements and this work is a popular one in both Indonesia and other countries.

Sometimes, this process of performance causes the audience to laugh and the performance space is filled with a lively atmosphere. In the fourth scene, the dancer descends from the stage to the auditorium and shakes hands with members of the audience. There are shouts of delight from the audience as the seating area becomes part of the performance. His popularity is evident from such reactions to his performance.

In his own comments about this work he says that he wants to show how in the modern dances of Indonesia there is much influence from foreign countries such as China, India, and to some extent, from Western countries.

This showcases his disagreement with the essentialized interpretation of "Chineseness". He focuses on the "Indonesia-ness" as opposed to the "Chinese-ness" and shows that what is called "Indonesian dance" contains various cultural elements from other traditions. What "Indonesian dance" is should be considered, together with what "Chinese-ness" is.

Didik is devoted to performing a range of Asian dances, and also Western dances. The supreme skill and original devices he reveals are remarkable. He expresses his own identity as a dancer through respect for a variety of Asian dance traditions. This indication of multiple Asian elements is his own way of displaying resistance to the essentialism that focuses on one single identity.

---

13 *Dangdut* is a genre of Indonesian popular music based on Malay music (*orkes Melayu*). Rhoma Irama, known as the founder of this music, integrated the musical style of Indian film songs, Arabic music, and rock music with Malay music. He established a genre termed *dangdut* in the 1970s.

Highlights of *Panca Sari*

In this work, the audience can enjoy Didik's entertaining talents as a dancer and a comedian. After the performance of a Chinese dance using a long ribbon, the dancer entertains the audience through comical Javanese dancing and acting in the second scene. Subsequently, the dancer shows his skillful modern street dancing by wearing a gold-colored shop-bought mask in the third scene. Wearing a Balinese mask, the dancer likens himself to a marionette and performs skillful movements in the fourth scene. In the final scene, when the dancer is dressed in a red costume, he turns the face of a monkey mask to the audience and the auditorium fills with laughter.

The dancer's interaction with the audience is one of the most prominent characteristics of this work.

© Hitoshi Furuya, Gudo, East Java, 2011: The final scene of *Panca Sari*, performing a comical play with *dangdut* music while wearing a monkey mask in a Chinese temple

4

From Comedy to Serious Performance: The Creative Work
Dewi Sarak Jodag

4-1
Comedian

Didik has become well known in Indonesia as a comedian. He has said that comedy is a skill only achieved by those who have mastered serious dance. He also makes an interesting comparison: "It is much like expert lawyers conning people using the law". For this reason, he has mastered the existing serious dance genres. In the interview he says that "having fully mastered the rules and spirit of traditional dance, the dancer reaches a point where he can then apply them to make his own style and develop comedic works".

Comedy is popular in Indonesia, audiences enjoy even a small comic twist, which makes for lively performances. Didik has often appeared on TV since the 1980s, and has performed comedy in dramas referred to as *sinetron*, and he has now become a household name. There are other actors who focus on the pursuit of laughs, but Didik handles comedy with sincerity. He believes graceful movements, beautiful costumes and makeup, and a high level of technique cannot be compromised, even in comedy.

Negative images held by society regarding male actors playing female roles are not unrelated to the fact that the majority of Didik's creative works prior to 2000 were comedies. Negative connotations attached to cross-dressers

© Hitoshi Furuya,
Candi Ratu Boko near Yogyakarta:
Shooting children's singing

© Didik Nini Thowok Entertainment,
Yogyakarta: A comedic play with
Wawin Lawura on a TV program

such as the *waria* or *banci* are not unrelated either[14]. Didik is aware that there were deep negative opinions existing in society. Despite audiences expressing admiration during a performance, upon the completion of the show some would shout insults at him as he left the theater (Mrázek 2005: 264). Since he knew that negative opinions existed, he made efforts to make audiences laugh while he played female roles in his creative works. Immediately after demonstrating his excellent dancing skills, he would change his wardrobe while facing away from the audience on the stage, and he made the audience laugh by exposing underwear attached to his back. He would remove the wig to reveal his shaved head, drawing further laughter from the audience. This was as if to purposely appeal to the folly of men playing roles for women. It was a strategic attempt of his deconstruction of gender stereotypes through comical acts. He emphasizes the comical dimension of his works

© Didik Nini Thowok Entertainment: A scene of the pop promotion

© HITOSHI FURUYA, 2004: Performing a comical play in collaboration with the Japanese group of *gamelan*, Lambangsari

[14] These negative connotations are also affected by the various informations on cross gender from the outside world, especially by Western "drag queens". However we should consider the differences between the Western "drag" and Indonesian concept of "cross gender". Hughes-Freeland also noted that Didik's performances needed to be analysed in relation to local contexts and culturally defined spheres (Hughes-Freeland 2008: 7–33).

by showing his excellent acting skills and by utilizing negative images of transgender dancers.

Didik wanted to perform serious dances instead of comedy. He desired to showcase his ability as a traditional dancer, and overcome the preconception in Indonesia that male dancers who assume female roles are comedians. However, in order to make a living from the stage, it is, of course, necessary to please the audiences. Serious female impersonating dancers have not always been appreciated in Indonesia. It is a difficult decision to make whether one chooses comedy or serious performance.

Although he had worked mainly as a comedian in Indonesia, the direction of his activities changed in 2000. He began to perform serious works on international stages. Through these international activities, Didik discovered the importance of female-impersonating dancers in other Asian countries.

4-2

Encountering Japanese *Onnagata* (Female-Role Players)

Didik came to Japan in 1999 and, as a Japan Foundation fellow, he studied *noh* plays and traditional Japanese dance. Through this experience, performances of Japanese *onnagata* (male actors who specialize in female roles) left a strong impression on Didik. He was much influenced by artists who attempt to achieve perfection in their roles, audiences who worship the achievement of these performers, and the solid existence of the genre known as *onnagata*. The existence of *onnagata* in Japanese classical performing arts made him determined to create a new flavor in his own work.

In a creative work entitled *Bedhaya Hagoromo*, he attempted to fuse the Javanese court dance *bedhaya* with the *Hagoromo* dance of Japanese *noh*. As well as learning of the existence of *onnagata* artists of Japan, he also met female-impersonating dancers from China, India, and many other Asian countries on his travels overseas. A question artists of other countries asked Didik was "Why do you perform female roles as comedy?" In these countries, many of these female roles are serious ones and he realized that this is a tradition that the artists painstakingly work to achieve. Experiences of meeting *onnagata* artists from other countries gave Didik an opportunity to rethink his own performances. There is no equivalent translation of *onnagata* in Java. He proposed the concept of "cross-gender", and has attempted to work with many artists from other Asian countries since 2000.

© Naoya Ikegami: Performance of *Hagoromo* dance of Japanese *noh*

4-3
Serious Work *Dewi Sarak Jodag*

The subject of the creative work entitled *Dewi Sarak Jodag* is Javanese tales of the romance of Panji. The lead character of this dance work, Sarak Jodag, disguises herself to hide her ugliness, and approaches the prince, Panji Asmarabangun. However, she lets her guard down and her true appearance is revealed. With shame and anger, Sarak Jodag dances fiercely. To express anger in the end, Didik created a new mask that was inspired by the Japanese *noh* mask "Hannya". The bright red mask was specially ordered from a Javanese mask maker, and a commercially available black wig was added. It expressed the violent anger of a woman whose true form had been revealed.

In the latter half, where the original red mask inspired by *noh* masks is used, a masculine masked dance is used to express the woman's fury. This was based on the dance of the masked devil from Cirebon, which he learned in the 1970s. Didik was asked if expressing a woman's fury in such fierce movements was characteristic of a male dancer

© Didik Nini Thowok Entertainment:
The dance of "anger" in *Dewi Sarak Jodag*

expressing "femininity". His answer to this question was unexpected. He responded that he borrowed the "masculine" expression from a female master from whom he had learned the masked dance. He performed the "masculinity" of a female master as a male dancer performing a female role. This shows his conviction that one can create "a female-role dancer's body" meant to express "femininity". It is a complex expression of gender only achieved by experienced female-role dancers.

The entire play is approximately 20 minutes in length. During that time he continually dances three types of dance while changing three masks and wigs. This requires an enormous level of endurance. The shape of original masks inspired by Japanese masks is incorporated in the Javanese dance expressions in the third scene. With inspiration from different cultures, he is always seeking frontiers for new expression.

During the play, in the scene of Sarak Jodag's courtship, Didik himself recorded lines that were played along with the background music. Her desperation makes the audience laugh. However, as in the entire play, the seriousness of the work, provided through the expressions on the three different masks, is clearly felt. This was his first serious work, completely different from his past comedic works. It could be seen as the first step towards his goal and was influenced by other Asian nations' expressions of "cross-gender".

Highlights of *Dewi Sarak Jodag*

The appeal of this play is the gradual changes in characters. In the first scene, when Sarak Jodag appears as Panji's beautiful lover, audiences can enjoy Didik's skill in playing a female character's grace and beauty, which is portrayed using elements from Javanese classical dance. In the second part, where he plays Sarak Jodag while wearing a comical mask, dynamic choreography based on folk dance can be seen. Dynamic and agile dances are Didik's forte, and these dances are fully utilized in this scene. In the middle of the music, there is a recording made by Didik of Sarak Jodag calling out to Panji. Such a performance provides a glimpse of his talent as a comedian. The highlight is, of course, the third scene with its fierce dance, depicting out of control fury. This play allows the audience to appreciate Didik's talent and technique because he performs three contrasting characters.

©Hitoshi Furuya, Tokyo, 2006: The first act of *Dewi Sarak Jodag*

© Hitoshi Furuya, Tokyo, 2006: A performance of Sarak Jodag

Column 4
Javanese Panji Romance

The Tale of Panji refers to a series of stories dating from the late 15th century, from eastern Java, that feature Prince Panji. The story follows Prince Panji of Koripan's (or Jenggala) journeys in search of his fiancée, the princess Candra Kirana (or Sekar Taji) of Daha (Kediri). During their journeys, the protagonist and the heroine disguise their social positions, use aliases and go through many wars and adventures to be ultimately united. However, there are stories of women who pretend to be the heroine in order to seduce the prince. Sarak Jodag in Didik's story is one of these women. The uniqueness of his dance work was that it focuses on Sarak Jodag, who was traditionally a villain, and depicts her emotions and humanity. This, again, is a unique characteristic of Didik's expression of femininity.

© Hitoshi Furuya, Tokyo, 2006: Performing "anger" in *Dewi Sarak Jodag*

5

As an Indonesian Dancer

5-1
As a Chinese Indonesian Artist

Didik himself attached importance to his identity as an Indonesian artist, not an artist of Chinese descent in his discourse. The Suharto era that had oppressed Chinese culture ended in 1998. Since the resignation of Suharto, Chinese culture began to be widely known in public society.

However, he feels that it is difficult to come to terms with the history of oppression, and he is conscious not to forget history.

On the other hand, in his cultural experience, the tradition of Javanese dance that has become part of him is proof of his identity as a dancer.

As a *peranakan* (Chinese Indonesian) dancer who was born in Indonesia, Didik has the determination to contribute to the development of arts in Indonesia. In most cases, the native tongue of the *peranakan* people is Indonesian, but they also use the regional language of the area in which they are raised. They are devoted to the tradition of art in their home region. Didik pays attention to the various Javanese art traditions and cultural concepts. Additionally, he desires to be a specialist who masters Javanese dance better than a true-born Javanese.

Moreover, he said that he will contribute as an Indonesian dancer. This means that he will be active not only

© Hitoshi Furuya, 2013:
Practice of Chinese traditional dance

© Hitoshi Furuya, 2013:
Celebrating a calligrapher, Sidik (center) together with Bernie Liem the president of the Friendly Organization between Germany and Indonesia (left)

as a Javanese dancer but also as an Indonesian dancer. Through his artistic activity, Didik wants to deviate from the image that Indonesians have of the Chinese community as people only associated with business, commerce, and economy, and wants to show that the Chinese descendants are also artists who can contribute to the cultural dimension of Indonesia.

In the fields of literature, theater, music, and the film industry, many artists of Chinese descent have contributed to Indonesia. Didik wants to be a pioneer in the field of dancing art as a representative artist of Indonesia.

5-2

Network of Chinese Descendant Communities

The wide network among Chinese people is also one of the important elements for Didik's performance activities. At the individual level, many friends ask him to perform at wedding ceremonies, at events for business corporations, etc. Also, there is the relationship with journalists and other artists. Occasionally, Didik can build a network at an event at a Chinese temple, where many Chinese people assemble. Although Didik himself is a Christian, he occasionally participates in events in Chinese temples (*klenteng*). In the event for the Chinese New Year in 2011, he performed one of his works and met the members of a Chinese puppet theater, or *wayang potehi*. Didik became acquainted with a Chinese merchant who was the leader of the puppet group, and Didik was impressed by the merchant's devotion to the artistic activity both as a member and as a patron. Didik mentioned that people should know there are many Chinese people contributing to the development of Indonesian arts.

After taking this opportunity, in September 2011 in Gudo, East Java, he was asked to perform at an event celebrating the commemoration of the building of a Chinese temple named Hong Sang Kiong (鳳山宮).

Along with Didik's network of Javanese or other Indonesian artists, and his connections with artists overseas, his network with Chinese friends is one of the most important elements of his artistic activities.

5-3
The Chinese Temple in Gudo, East Java

In the Chinese temple, Hong Sang Kiong, in Gudo, East Java, people celebrated the anniversary of its foundation in September 2011. Auspicious persons from various regions of Java island assembled there bringing statues of their chief gods. An extensive reception ceremony was then held for them. As each group arrived from the temples of other regions, an announcement of their name was made, and a music performance and lion dance were performed for them. During the event, the statues of the chief gods from various regions were placed inside this temple, and many people prayed to them. The solemn atmosphere inside the temple was quite different from the lively sounds at the gate of the temple. Inside the gate, there were many sacred palanquins and musical instruments that were to be used in the parade on the following day, and the area was crowded with many visitors and members of the temple preparing for the procession. The temple in Gudo is very spacious, and in addition to the main temple, there are

©HITOSHI FURUYA, Gudo, East Java, 2011: The Chinese temple "Hong Sang Kiong". People welcoming the statues of god from another temple

© Hitoshi Furuya, Gudo, East Java, 2011:
Praying in the Chinese temple

© Hitoshi Furuya, Gudo, East Java, 2011:
Inside of the Chinese temple

© Hitoshi Furuya, Gudo, East Java, 2011:
A musical band in the Chinese temple

© Hitoshi Furuya, Gudo, East Java, 2011:
The auction of a gold necklace in the Chinese temple

many facilities inside, such as the temple dedicated to Kwan-in（観音）and prayer areas, meeting rooms, accommodation areas, a huge hall, and kitchens.

The main god of the temple, Kuang Tse Tsun Wang, is the god of trade or migrant worker（廣澤尊王, 郭聖王）. The president of the famous cigarette company, Gudang Garam, who is said to have received a blessing from the main god, donated some spaces in this temple.

In the main kitchen, the meals for hundreds of people were cooked and were served to the guests in the meeting rooms.

Many people also ate outside the building. There were various kinds of dishes, such as vegetarian, Indonesian, and Chinese. The staff of the temple were busy serving the guests and managing the office work.

In the evening, Didik began to prepare for his performance. He began to put on makeup in his accommodation near the temple, talking with friends and instructing the staff in his company. After finishing putting on makeup, he donned his costume and topknot. In the next room, his coactor, a magician, prepared for his performance. After the preparation, both of them sat together and discussed advance arrangements of the program for the night's skits. It was not a rehearsal for the acting, but they discussed and exchanged ideas with each other quietly, and confirmed the program.

The performance on the night began with a singing contest and karaoke music. Accompanying the singing was the performance of a live band and there was also colorful lighting. After the audience enjoyed the karaoke session, at approximately eight o'clock, Didik arrived at the temple. Didik's entrance in the temple was welcomed by the audience's cry of "Nini Thowok!" Many fans came backstage and asked if they could take a photograph with him.

As the last performer, he danced one of his original works, entitled *Panca Sari*. He expressed the five different elements involved in comedic acts. After the performance, his magician friend appeared onstage and they performed some magic, sang, and acted in some comical skits.

Didik, as a skillful singer, sang a short folk song alternating Javanese, Western, and Mandarin styles, receiving applause from the audience. The musical band also adapted

© Hitoshi Furuya, Gudo, East Java, 2011:
Talking with the magician, Wisben, about the program for the day

© Hitoshi Furuya, Gudo, East Java, 2011: Performing a comical play

5 As an Indonesian Dancer

to his ad-lib singing and played accompaniment to his songs. After the performance, Didik and his magician friend held an auction of a gold necklace to obtain funds for the operation of the temple.

Some of the members of the operating organization of this temple are Chinese gold merchants. They offered some gold necklaces to help raise funds for the temple. The participants from the various regions made bids for the items.

Didik went around to the participants, showing them the gold necklace, and the bids made rose as a result of his popularity. Three auctions, conducted with much enthusiasm, were the final events of the night before the people returned to their homes.

After the event, many security guards at the site of the temple came up to Didik and asked for a photograph with him.

One of the committee members of the temple, Mr. T, is a descendant of a Chinese *wayang potehi* puppet theater player. Although he did not take over the puppet theater, he made efforts to develop it, supporting the purchase of musical instruments, the making of puppets and the training of performers. At the time of writing, all of the members of this puppet troupe are Javanese. Didik had learned of Mr. T and his efforts when the puppet group performed at a Chinese temple in Yogyakarta.

Didik, as a dancer who has made efforts to feature both

© MADOKA FUKUOKA, Gudo, East Java, 2011:
Talking picture with the guards in the Chinese temple

Javanese and Indonesian dancing in his original works, was impressed by Mr. T's activities in supporting the development of the puppet theater.

Aside from the performance in Chinese temple, Didik also performs at wedding parties or manages the production of large-scale events at the request of the Chinese entrepreneur. Didik's network of Chinese people is one of the important elements that support his performances.

5-4
Chinese New Year in Yogyakarta

In February 2013, in Yogyakarta, which is the base of Didik's artistic activity, an event entitled Yogyakarta Chinese Cultural Week was held. This event was the celebration of the 15th day of the Chinese New Year. And, on this occasion, also included the formal announcement of the construction of a gate for the Chinatown.

This was the 8th anniversary event to be held, and was called "Sewindu Pekan Budaya Tionghoa Yogyakarta". This title was derived from the Javanese word *windu*, which means a cycle of eight years. In the entrance of the old Chinatown, located in the center of Yogyakarta city, the beautiful gate

© MADOKA FUKUOKA, Yogyakarta, 2013: A collaboration with a calligrapher at the opening event of Yogyakarta Chinese Cultural Week

©Madoka Fukuoka, Yogyakarta, 2013: The gate at Ketandan

was constructed and, during the five-day event, many people went through this gate, walked around the Chinatown, and enjoyed seeing the stage performances and eating at the food stands.

Didik, as a member of the committee, helped manage this event, and he also performed a Chinese masked dance at the opening ceremony and an original work based on the Chinese white snake legend at the closing ceremony. This event became an occasion for merrymaking for the entire city. The mayor's wife, a Muslim, served as the chairperson, and the sultan of Yogyakarta attended the event.

Didik performed dances of Chinese origin, such as a Chinese masked dance and a work based on a Chinese legend, not his works based on Javanese dances. In this event, he attached importance to his performance of Chinese elements. Since the establishment of this Chinese cultural week, attention to the culture of Chinese people has been promoted. Didik had not featured the expression of Chinese elements as a Chinese descendant dancer until approximately 2010. However, in various kinds of opportunities of collaboration with the Chinese descendant communities, he has begun to feature Chinese elements in his performances. Although we are aware of these changes in his performances, we do not know if they are intentional on his part, or whether they are emerging from changes in his subconscious mind at this point in time.

© Madoka Fukuoka, Yogyakarta, 2013: A Chinese puppet play on a small stage

© MADOKA FUKUOKA, Yogyakarta, 2013: The opening event
on 19th February. Sultan Hamengkubuwono 10th's speech

© MADOKA FUKUOKA, Yogyakarta, 2013:
A New-Year display in a shopping mall in Yogyakarta

6

The Body of
a Female-
Impersonating
Dancer

6-1

Training the Body

Diet and yoga are Didik's secrets to controlling his body weight and shape. He eats many vegetables and fruits and reduces his intake of rice and other carbohydrates. He has maintained a slender body, looking much younger than his age. However, he said that since aged 50, controlling his body shape has gradually become more difficult. And he tends to put on weight, especially around the waist. The most problematic aspect of this is wearing tight costumes. In his performances, when the dancer needs to change a series of costumes one after another, wearing several layers of costumes at the outset is necessary. He needs to be careful not to get fat to ensure that his clothes do not become bundled up.

Aside from his body shape and weight, he also pays great attention to controlling the beauty of his appearance such as his well-toned skin and face. He states that, as a stage artist, it is important to maintain his appearance. Also, Didik continues to do yoga with his Indian master, not only for control of his body shape, but also to master breathing, especially abdominal breathing. Breathing brings contrast and life to dancing. Yoga is an important practice for concentrating the mind and controlling breathing. Didik always maintains gentle and graceful manners in his daily life; however, in his performance, he indicates the contrast of stillness and dynamics. He expresses refined elegance as well as the energy of violence or quick, amusing movements. Breathing techniques help him to express the dynamism of these changes in his performance.

MAKEUP: Skill in applying stage makeup is essential for a dancer. Before performing, Didik puts on the makeup of a beautiful woman's face, carefully using his cosmetic instruments. He paints long-slitted eyes, a straight nose, puts on eye shadow and eyelashes and makes a beautiful, feminine face. He has a preference for natural cosmetics, but he also often uses convenient items such as seal-type eye makeup from a one coin shop. He has explored original and practical ways of wearing makeup. In recent years, he has used farsighted glasses, a magnifying mirror, etc.

© Hitoshi Furuya, Yogyakarta, 2011: Putting on makeup before a performance

6 The Body of a Female-Impersonating Dancer

His method of wearing makeup is based on traditional Javanese makeup, which he mastered in his days at the academy. He is also a qualified makeup artist for traditional Javanese weddings. Makeup is one of the most important skills and knowledge required by Javanese dancers. As previously mentioned, the art institute holds classes for applying makeup, and Didik has also taught in these classes in his academy.

The technique of wearing makeup in Javanese dances has a close relationship with the epic or story world. To master the technique, the dancer should absorb much knowledge about the characters in the stories and master techniques to realize the appearance of these characters. Didik combined his original method of wearing makeup with the knowledge and techniques he had learned. In 2012, he published a book about makeup that documented his long term experience[15]. He is interested in various kinds of makeup in Asian countries such as in China, India, and Japan. In the old days in Java, old women used cosmetics made from rice flour. This was claimed to have good effects on the skin. As much as possible he adopts natural materials or ingredients that are believed to have good effects on the body.

WIG: He uses various kinds of wigs, and keeps his own hair short so that he can easily put on a wig for any character. His wig changes include those with a Javanese traditional bun,

© Didik Nini Thowok Entertainment: After finishing makeup

© Hitoshi Furuya: Makeup supplies

[15] The title of the book is *Stage Make Up: 25 Kreasi Make up untuk Pentas, Teater, Tari dan Film* (*Stage Make Up: 25 Creations of Make Up for Stage Performance, Theater, Dancing and Film*). The book was published by Gramedia Publishing.

long black hair, needle-shaped hair, and a bun of gray hair. As well as specially ordered wigs, he also uses wigs that are commercially avaliable. When he performs traditional dances, he uses traditional bun. He produces the feminine appearance of a Javanese woman using makeup and a bun. This style is also used for performing West Javanese dance or singing on the stage. When he performs Balinese female dances, he uses a headdress covering his head.

In the performance of his original works, he pays great attention to the combination of masks. In one of his original works, entitled *Dewi Sarak Jodag*, which was derived from the Javanese Panji tales, he uses an original red mask

© HITOSHI FURUYA: A topknot used for *Panca Sari*

to express the woman's anger. The wigs that are combined with the mask are ones with needle-like violet hair or black hair. In addition, he uses a bun of gray hair combined with the old woman mask, a shaggy wig combined with a clown mask, and topknots decorated with flowers for performing traditional Japanese and Chinese dances.

Being conscious of the important functions of wigs in the performance, Didik always tries to find surprising ways of using them. When he wears masks on both sides of his head, the mask and wigs are sometimes one piece.

COSTUME: Costume is one of the most important factors in dancing for transforming into a female character. Costumes sometimes restrict the dancer's body movements, but can also provide new possibilities for the movements.

Wearing undergarments is important for maintaining an appropriate "feminine" physique. When performing a classical female dance, it is important to dress and act "feminine". To be seen as a female, not only the costume but also the body must be transformed into a female form.

© HITOSHI FURUYA, Gudo, East Java, 2011: Singing with the magician, Wisben

Didik naturally has the appropriate physique and, through weight control and exercise, he has maintained an amazingly slim body. Under his stage costumes, he wears undergarments that help to accentuate feminine lines.

When he performed together with the Japanese *gamelan* group, *Lambangsari*, in 2004, he performed both a classical Central Javanese dance and a classical East Javanese dance. In both dances, the movements of the upper parts of the body were accentuated. Didik always looks perfect no matter what costume he is wearing.

VOICE AND SINGING: There are many opportunities for Didik to show his singing ability on the stage. Usually after the dance performance, Didik acts a short comical skit, sometimes with his co-player, and sings. In his singing, Didik does not always use a particularly "female" voice. He is a good singer in his natural voice. This is the result of his constant practice in vocalization and singing, and also his endeavors to explore various kinds of songs.

During his stay in Japan in 1999-2000, he had many opportunities to see performances of traditional Japanese theater as well as other types of stage theater. Through these experiences, he was influenced by the actors' original forms of vocalization. When he viewed performances in the Takarazuka theater, he was impressed by the male-role actress' methods of vocalization and interested in the way they care for their throats. He is interested in both dancing and singing, and in performances in Japan he often sings Japanese songs.

6-2

Devices for Transformation by Masks: Multiple Expressions of Gender

A particularly notable characteristic of Didik's creative performances is the frequent use of masks (Mrázek 2005: 254-261, Fukuoka 2014: 66). It is possible to transform oneself by altering facial appearance with makeup, but it is also time-consuming. Therefore a mask provides an excellent and effective solution that not only saves time but also enables the actor to become an instantly recognizable character.

Didik studied a mask dance in Cirebon, West Java, in the latter half of the 1970s. He apprenticed himself to Suji, a great dancer, in the Palimanan area and he learned the mask dance in the Palimanan style under Suji. The Cirebonese masked dance is based on a Panji romance that originated from East Java in approximately the 15th century. Performance styles of Cirebonese masked dances can be divided into two basic types. One of these is a masked drama style that involves enacting episodes from a Panji Romance story. The other style places an emphasis on expressing the nature of each mask by way of dance. In Cirebon, the main performance style is currently the latter. At present, it is only rarely that the enactment of stories through masked drama can be witnessed, for dance-centered masked performances now occupy the mainstream. The dancers wear five or six kinds of masks, one after another, proceeding from a *linyep* (refined) character through a number of stages to arrive at a *gagah* (rough) character.

His master, Suji, was known for exuding a charismatic aura on the stage as well as possessing great dancing skills.

©Didik Nini Thowok Entertainment: Three of the masks for *Dewi Sarak Jodag*

From his experience of learning under Suji, Didik mastered the expressions of the various characters indicated through the masks.

In later years, Didik also received tutelage from Sawitri in the Losari style, and from Rasinah in the Indramayu prefecture. Didik's teachers were all women who could play male characters extraordinarily well. Didik learned their skills and methods of displaying dynamic energy, roughness, and nimbleness. Based on these learning experiences, Didik perfectly mastered the use of various kinds of masks, and the impressions they create.

Some of the masks he uses in the performances are from his collection of masks from various regions, and some are custom-made. His order-made masks are usually from a maskmaker in the Bantul area, Supono, to whom he provides photographs or pictures of his ideas. By using various kinds of masks efficiently, he can achieve any impression he wants on the stage.

For example, in his popular work entitled *Panca Sari*, in the third scene, after performing a Javanese dance and a Chinese dance using a long ribbon, he uses a gold-colored shop-bought mask and performs robot movements based

© Didik Nini Thowok Entertainment:
The mask for the work *Bedhaya Hagoromo*

on street dancing.

Also, in the work entitled *Topeng Waran Kekek*, he uses three kinds of masks efficiently and performs as a beautiful woman, a comical hag, and an old woman.

In a creative work from 2004 entitled *Dewi Sarak Jodag*, Didik uses three kinds of masks: To expresses the elegant lover of Prince Panji, a comical hag who disguises herself as the prince's lover, and a furious woman after her true figure has been revealed. The third mask of this work, based on the Japanese "Hannya" masks from *noh* plays, expresses the anger and the devilishness of women. Didik ordered the mask from Supono, providing his idea for the work with a picture of a Japanese "Hannya" mask.

The masks used in Javanese mask dances are made of wood, with a piece of leather fastened to the inside surface so that the performer can grasp and support the mask in the mouth. As such, the performer is able to instantly put on the mask and be "transformed" more readily than is possible with masks placed over the head and held in place by string behind the head. The instant transformation produces dramatic effects in the performance.

The masks in traditional mask plays portray expressions for the characters, and these expressions are chosen from the characters' roles in the play. In Didik's works, there are both expressions that are faithful to the traditional expression, and expressions that deviate from typical ones associated with the characters. Occasionally, Didik intentionally adopts an expression that deviates from the expected image on the mask.

He also explores his own original expressions by giving new interpretations to shop-bought masks and custom-made masks[16].

His skills in producing these surprising expressions are derived from his original ideas and are also the result of his constant practice.

---

[16] There are many shop-bought masks in his collection. Also, he often orders original masks from a maskmaker, Supono, in Kasongan area, Bantul prefecture. There are many original masks in Didik's studio.

7

From the
Local Community
to the World

7-1

Teachers

Didik has studied dancing under many teachers. In the 1970s, he learned *topeng* Cirebon under the charismatic master Suji. He mastered *topeng* dancing while living under the same roof as the master. In East Java, Didik learned dance from the master of female-role dancing, Rasimun. In Bali, he studied under several teachers. He learned *legong* dance from the master in Saba region, I Gusti Gede Raka. In Japan, India, and China, he developed his skill under even more teachers. In Japan, he learned *noh* plays from Richard Emert, and Japanese dance from Masanosuke Gojo (Tamami Gojo). He also attaches great importance to the after-learning process. He periodically visits and meets his masters. Sometimes, he even performs together with his master. If one of his masters passes away, he visits the master's house and meets the family, and then visits the grave of the master. Didik is determined not to forget his own path to becoming an artist.

The secret to learning under various teachers is to regard himself as a complete beginner each time. In every place he has visited, he learned dance under various teachers. He empties himself and removes prejudice and stereotypes. He considers his fame in his country and his skills as a Javanese dancer as inconsequential. Through feeling he is nothing, he can learn new artistic traditions. He maintains his respect for the various kinds of artistic traditions in the world. Continually returning to his original aspirations might be the secret to keeping young.

7-2

An Artist in a Local Place

August 2007. On one Saturday evening, Didik performed a street performance on Malioboro Road in the center of Yogyakarta city. Around 5 p.m., many people had already assembled on the street to see his performance. Some of them said that Didik would arrive soon. In Yogyakarta people call him by the friendly title "Mas Didik". After waiting for a few moments, a truck playing music stopped at the roadside. Also, a car stopped on the other side of the road and Didik, wearing a female costume, got out. There were also other dancers getting out of other cars. Didik wore a Javanese top made of bright green-yellow colored fabric. He was wearing a wig with a Javanese topknot and sunglasses that he had bought in a fashion goods store in Shinjuku, Tokyo. Didik and his staff danced accompanied by recorded music from a speaker. Many people gathered around the space and enjoyed the performance. In Java, a street performance is called *ngamen*. Some people make a living in this way. In the case of street performances by a famous artist such as Didik, it is possible to attract a large audience. Didik holds street performances to collect donations. Yogyakarta was damaged by an earthquake in May 2006. After the disaster, many children experienced great difficulties. The street performance on that Saturday evening was held to collect donations for an orphanage. After finishing the performance, the audience members asked Didik if they could take photographs with him, using their cellphones. Didik accepted their requests and the

© Didik Nini Thowok Entertainment:
Dance performance in Semarang, Central Java

taking of photographs continued for about an hour. Although he has many opportunities to perform concerts abroad and in other large towns in Indonesia, Didik always pays great attention to his local area, communicating directly with the residents and returning the fruits of his artistic activities to them.

After the earthquake in East Japan in March 2011, he held some charity performances in various regions of Java and sent the money he gathered to the disaster-stricken area. Japan is one place that is full of memories for him because he often has the opportunity to perform in Japan and he has learned traditional Japanese dances. His relationship

© MADOKA FUKUOKA, Yogyakarta, 2007:
The street performance in Malioboro Road

with local residents and his concern for their well-being are the motivations behind staging these activities.

7-3
Performances in Various Regions of the World

Having had many opportunities to perform abroad, Didik is a popular and famous dancer outside of Indonesia. He has many opportunities to visit and perform abroad. He performs in Japan almost annually. In his performances abroad, he is sometimes accompanied by staff, but occasionally he performs alone. He has also spent a month in Europe, traveling to various countries there, with his suitcase carrying his costumes and masks. He is active and mobile, and not restricted by his fame in his homeland. When in Japan he enjoys Japanese foods such as *ramen*, *shabu-shabu*, and *mentaiko*. Although he sometimes restricts the amount of food he eats in order to control his weight, he always enjoys eating and talking with various Japanese people. In 2006, Didik joined a project named "Nanyo Kagura", (*kagura* in the South Seas)[17] which included a Japanese musician,

Article from the newspaper *Warta Jateng* from 9th April 2011:
"Didik Nini Thowok collects 3, 5 million rupiah in one hour"

[17] *Kagura* is a traditional Japanese theatrical play. It is performed with sacred Shinto music and dance and in many cases it is performed in a shrine.

Kei Wada, and a Japanese dancer, Tetsuro Koyano. Wada and Koyano, through experience of learning music and dance in Bali, had designed a project where masked actors use a minimum of words. The stage directions, shadow puppets, music, and the mask play are influenced by the traditional performing art forms of Bali. The characteristics of this project and the featured expressions of the masks used are common to Didik's form of artistic expression. Through the course of several performances, Didik played various kinds of roles. Through practice with

©Madoka Fukuoka, 2013: A rehearsal of "Nanyo Kagura"

Japanese musicians, dancers, actors, he formed unique collaborations. Although, sometimes, there were difficulties in verbal communication, he drew on his talent to understand and feel the intentions of the other members, and produced his original aura on the stage. Koyano regards Didik's intuition, skill, and beauty very highly. The performances met with much appreciation from the Japanese audiences.

Didik has many friends all over Japan. He has visited Tokyo, Osaka, Nagoya, and Kyushu to see friends and hold workshops or give performances. During his stays, he conducts fieldwork in the regions he visits and collects data about traditional performing arts and stories or myths. Additionally, he observes the full range of Japanese performances from classical, traditional to popular. Curiosity and activeness are at the base of his creative activity. In so many places of the world his friends await his visits and performances.

In 2001, Didik received a subsidy from the Japan Foundation and collaborated with Asian female-role artists on a program named "*onnagata* tour". Through this project, he got to know artists from various regions, such as India, China, and Korea. He also joined the Asia Pacific Performing Arts Network (APPAN). The members of this network have held annual seminars and performances in their own countries in turn.

© MADOKA FUKUOKA, Tokyo, 2007: A dance workshop with Tetsuro Koyano at Aoyama Gakuin University

© Hitoshi Furuya, Malaysia: A performance of *Siddartha*, arranged by his friend Alex Dea

In 2004, Didik held an event which he named "cross-gender" in Yogyakarta to celebrate his 50th birthday, which included artistic performances by many artists. In 2009, he participated in a performance event for APPAN in Yokohama.

Since 2016, Didik has participated in the theatrical project held by Japanese NPO corporation of theatrical creation, "Za Koenji", in Tokyo. It is the serial project, entitled "One Table Two Chairs" where the artists from the Asian countries create some collaborative theatrical plays, using one table and two chairs as the shared stage setting. The project is directed by Makoto Sato and coordinated by Yoshiro Hatori with the hope of transcending the various kinds of cultural boundaries and constructing the free space of creative activities.

In October 2016, Didik created a collaborative work with Sun Yi Jun, an actress of Chinese theater Kūnqǔ (崑曲). The work was directed by Danny Yun, a stage director from Hong Kong.

Also in October 2017, at the moment of proofreading of this writing, Didik is preparing another theatrical play for the same event doing collaboration with a male actor of Kūnqǔ, Wang Bin. The work is directed by Liu Xiaoyi, a stage director from Singapore.

© HITOSHI FURUYA, Tokyo, 2016: Performance in "One Table Two Chairs" at "Za Koenji"

8

As a Manager
of a Studio,
as a Teacher

8-1
Education of Staff

Didik founded his own dance studio "Natya lakshita", in 1980 and uses modern methods to manage it. As of 2012, there were 10 members of staff in the studio. Some are the members of his dance company, and some are support staff for studio management, such as assistants to the performers, the staff who arrange the schedules, the dancers, the teachers of dance classes and costume, finance, documentation, and data-gathering staff. Although Didik manages the studio in a modern way, for him the studio staff are like a family who work together and eat together. He has a two-story studio on Godean street in the northwest area of Yogyakarta[18]. On the first floor he has his own office and works there every day. He keeps contact with many people around the world on his mobile phone and computer. He holds negotiations about performances abroad, discussions with researchers and creates advertisements for performances, etc., using email and some social network services. Sometimes, he holds meetings with the office staff and teaches and inspects the practices in the studio on the second floor. In his house, which is located near the office, he has a space for dance practice and a room for his dance costumes, and teaches students and arranges various preparations for performances.

© HITOSHI FURUYA: Teaching dance in the studio

© HITOSHI FURUYA: Children's class in studio

[18] At the moment of proofreading of this writing, 2017, Didik already moved his studio from Godean to the new space in the backyard of his house in Jatimulyo. Also he is preparing to join the management of another art space in an art village located in Kulon Progo, the West part of Yogyakarta to be named "Nusantara Art Village" ("Kampung Seni Nusantara")

© Hitoshi Furuya: Didik's dance studio in Godean,
in the northwest of Yogyakarta city

8 As a Manager of a Studio, as a Teacher

© Hitoshi Furuya: Preparing for a performance

© Hitoshi Furuya, 2011: Giving an interview to the students of a junior high school

© Madoka Fukuoka, 2012: Staff in his studio wearing uniforms. The red uniforms are worn on Mondays

© Hitoshi Furuya, 2013: Meeting with staff in his studio

© Hitoshi Furuya, 2013: The dance studio in his home

© Madoka Fukuoka, 2012: The nameplate of the dance studio in Didik's house

8-2
Composition of Works

Didik constantly creates new works. There are various motivations behind his creations. In some cases, there are his experiences in foreign countries, inspiration he acquires from unique individuals he meets, and inspiration from the appearances of masks.

In 2006, I sent a Japanese *Izumo kagura* mask of "Kushinadahime", to him. I thought it would be better used in a creative work than simply being a decoration in the entrance of my house. After several months, Didik sent the news about his new work. It was a fusion work featuring the Javanese story of the goddess of rice paddies, Dewi Sri, and the Japanese *Izumo kagura* mask. At the beginning, the dancer wears an original costume derived from a Japanese *kimono*, a wig of long silver hair, and this mask. He has developed this work, as well as the appearance of the dancer, several times.

Didik often gets inspiration from masks for his original choreography, as well as from the classical or folk dances of various regions. For example, he invited a young dancer and drum player of *jaipongan* dance from West Java to teach him the dance techniques and then made a documentary recording of this. Similarly, for the *lengger* dance of the Banyumas region, he also invited a young dancer to his

© Didik Nini Thowok Entertainment: A collaboration with a Javanese puppeteer and another Asian musician

▶ © HITOSHI FURUYA, 2011: A collaboration with a Japanese instrument, *koto* player while wearing the Kushinadahime mask

© HITOSHI FURUYA: Playing the role of Ardhanareesvara, the androgynous form of Siva, from Hindu myth. Didik wears the asymmetric costume and mask on his back

INDONESIAN CROSS-GENDER DANCER DIDIK NINI THOWOK

© Hitoshi Furuya: Didik puts the asymmetric makeup on his front

home and learned the dance technique. If the dancers are really skilled experts, Didik asks them to teach him, even though they are younger than him. Also, he provides members of his company with the opportunity to have lessons and learn dances from these experts.

Through these various learning experiences, he incorporates the elements that he studies into his original works. By doing so, he establishes original methods for creating works. His method is similar to an arrangement of accessories taken from a full jewelry box.

He does not compromise when making music and sounds for his performances. Usually he uses edited recordings. For recording he sometimes employs excellent musicians from other parts of Indonesia and makes elaborate musical compositions. The specialist technical staff in his studio play an important role in this process. They make several versions of one work, such as a 15-minute version, a 10-minute version, etc. Didik then utilizes these edited recordings for various performances over many occasions.

In September 2011, the members of his company practiced in the studio for the opening event of an international conference on gender that was held at Gajah Mada University in Yogyakarta. The dancers to play female roles were selected through auditions that Didik held in his studio. The final selections included approximately 10 members, including students of the National Arts Institute. Didik arranged the work using folk dances from the Banyumas region, West Javanese *jaipongan*, and the dances of the Batak people from Sumatra. He produced all of the elements of the work including choreography, music, costumes, and masks. He arranged the times for practice and rehearsal in his schedule. Didik also performs the dance of the Hindu god, Ardhanareesvara, in this work. To express the androgynous figure of the god, he devised asymmetrical makeup for the right and left sides of his face and an asymmetrical costume for the right and left sides of his body. Also, he performs the dance using his back and front, wearing a mask on the back of his head.

The Next Generation

When I asked Didik about his plans for the next generation, he asked me "For which followers?" He has many students in his dance studio and also many able staff members. However, he differentiates between the dances that he teaches to his students and the dances that he uses for performing. The dances that he performs he keeps secret and maintains personal control over them, therefore he teaches his students other dances. Hence, he does not encounter much competition in his field. He said that he got the idea for this approach from the manner in which a famous Javanese chicken restaurant protects the names of its secret ingredients. This method has something in common with a transmission method of Japanese traditional performing arts called *isshi soden*, in which the master teaches his/her secret arts to only a legitimate heir. However, there is still the problem of who should be the heir to his arts. A very talented dancer with a beautifully proportioned body would be required to continue the performance of Didik's original works. However, having talent and a beautiful body alone is not sufficient. More important is that the person should have integrity, and be someone who can maintain respect for various kinds of artistic traditions and masters. It is a style that an unparalleled dancer constructed in his generation. This is different from the long-term construction of classical art forms. In his own style, the important factors are the original ideas and amazing abilities of an individual dancer. Firstly, we need to consider if there is a necessity for a successor. If it is necessary, are there any appropriate candidates to succeed Didik's original mastery?

© Didik Nini Thowok Entertainment:
A picture for promotion

9

The 2014
Event REBORN

Didik commemorated his 60th birthday in December 2014 and held a three-day event he called "'REBORN'[19]: International Dance Performance and Seminar" in Yogyakarta city. This event showed that there are diverse traditions of men playing female roles in Asian nations, and it was an opportunity for him to dedicate a compilation of his own creative works to the sultan, the King of Yogyakarta, and also to continue his artistic activity as a mature dancer. The event began on December 4th with the performance of an Eastern Javanese masked dance, *topeng* Malang, and a popular drama, *ludruk*. During the morning of December 5th, an international seminar on cross-gender in Asia was held. In the evenings of the 5th and 6th, there were dance performances in the outdoor theater located in the town center. This venue is a large pavilion called a *pendapa*, consisting of a stone floor and pillars built on land. This pavilion belongs to the royal family and is named "Bangsal Kepatihan". On the evening of the 5th, cross-gender (mainly female impersonation) performances from

© MADOKA FUKUOKA, Yogyakarta, 2014: Seminar

[19] The name "REBORN" is derived from the Chinese and Japanese *kanreki* by which a person's zodiac status restarts after he/she reaches 60 years of age.

© Madoka Fukuoka, Yogyakarta, 2014: Masked dance of Malang

© Madoka Fukuoka, Yogyakarta, 2014: A scene from *Ludruk* performance

© Madoka Fukuoka, Yogyakarta, 2014: *Onnagata* performance

© Madoka Fukuoka: *Onnagata* performance

© Madoka Fukuoka: *Bedhaya Hagoromo*

different areas of Indonesia and from other Asian nations were presented. On the evening of the 6th, *Bedhaya Hagoromo* was performed, which was co-created by Didik and his fellow performers with inspiration from Japanese *noh* plays and Javanese court dancing.

There were many good reviews as well as some negative criticisms of this event. Specifically, holders of some events with the term "cross-gender" in the titles, were under pressure to change the titles, and some venues cancelled the performances. Indonesia has the highest Muslim population in the world, and is often critical of cross-gender or transgender expressions, including men performing female roles. However, many cross-gender dance performances attract large audiences at the event. In Yogyakarta city, which was the center of royal culture that originated

© MADOKA FUKUOKA: *Onnagata* performance

© Madoka Fukuoka: Cross gender performance from East Java ... o X and Yogyakarta by Didik Nini Thowok

© Madoka Fukuoka: Performance of *Bedhaya Hagoromo*

© Madoka Fukuoka: Performance of *wayang wong gunung* from Magelang near from Yogyakarta

from cultural traditions of the Hindu-Java era, people have much interest in various kinds of art performances, and the public is often seen enjoying dance performances. All performances of the event lasted for three hours or more, without an intermission; yet, often the atmosphere was passionate and cheers and applause continued long into the night. Meanwhile, during the performance in a solemn atmosphere on the night of the 6th, the audience that filled the venue held its breath in quiet seriousness.

Through this event, Didik may have succeeded in solidifying his performances as a compilation of the diverse traditions of female-impersonating dances across Asia.

© MADOKA FUKUOKA: Presenting the document of *Bedhaya Hagoromo* to Sultan Hamengkubuwono 10th

Afterword

Afterword: Madoka Fukuoka

In September 2011, I visited Yogyakarta with my friend, the photographer Hitoshi Furuya. Our purpose was to see Didik Nini Thowok and his performances, to conduct an interview, and to take some photographs of him. Both of us know Didik well but it was the first time for us to meet with him together. We were considering the possibility of making a book about this unique dancer and after discussing this several times, we travelled to Yogyakarta.

On September 16th, we went to the Gudo region of East Java with Didik Nini Thowok, who was scheduled to perform in an event to mark the anniversary of the foundation of the Chinese temple there. Right until departure, the dancers in his studio practiced for the performance, which had been scheduled for the coming October. For the event, Didik had held auditions in the studio at his home. Holding these auditions was an opportunity for Didik to discover talented dancers. He invited masters of dance from East and West Java, learned their skills, and took the opportunity to learn together with his staff. Through these processes he created a new work, adopting elements of music and dancing from the various regions. He designed costumes and took part in the process of making them. Usually he produces all of the aspects of his creative works and his staff support him. At the

©Hitoshi Furuya, September 2011: A practice in the studio at his home

practices in the studio, he carefully checked the choreography and the stage floor layout. Although he did not compromise on the quality and checked every detail, he was always calm when discussing with his staff and dancers. His personality remained that of the mild-mannered, refined dancer we know. There were many guests visiting his home so, in the intermission of the practice, he received them and took our interview. The staff were traveling there from Didik's studio and home by motorcycle and reported to him the matters of the dance studio. Didik always had a mobile phone with him and checked his e-mail regularly. It was an opportunity for me to catch a glimpse of his busy daily life as an artist and also as the owner of his studio.

After finishing all preparations and hospitality for the guests, we departed for Gudo at night. The journey takes approximately seven hours by car. We arrived at a house with several rooms that was owned by one of the staff members of the temple. The next morning after taking a nap, we walked around the neighborhood. Many people talked with Didik and asked for pictures with him. He didn't show any tiredness and met with all of his fans there. Also, he enjoyed the special products of the Gudo region, such as small mangos and large Tapioka crackers and chatted with the local people.

At the Chinese temple in Gudo, Didik met with a variety of people, including the staff of the temple. After that, he walked around the site and looked at the various activities in progress.

© Hitoshi Furuya, Gudo, East Java, 2011

Returning to the accommodation, he began to prepare for the night's performance. He put on his makeup carefully, as well as his costumes, and held preliminary discussions with his co-performing magician. He also chatted with his staff while he made careful preparations. He gave instructions to the staff about recording the performance. After finishing the preparation, we went to the temple again. The people around there called out to him "Nini Thowok!" Many people visited his dressing room and asked for pictures with him.

The program for the performance was *Panca Sari*. It is one of his most famous works and expresses the five elements of comedic acts. After finishing the dances, he and the magician performed magic and comical plays, and sang. At the end, they auctioned three gold pendants as the final event of the night. After that the audience returned home.

The next day we returned to Yogyakarta by train. Many people who met us at the station and in the train talked to Didik and took pictures with him. The conductor of the train suddenly began to dance after seeing Didik and talked with him. People came up to Didik and spoke to him, and he always pleasantly responded. After getting off the train at the station in Yogyakarta, many people, including the driver of a rickshaw, asked him "Where have you come from, Mas Didik?" "What kind of shooting were you doing?" etc. Local people welcomed the popular Yogyakarta artist.

On the three-day trip we were always accompanied by one of his female friends who is also a dancer and he talked with her often. She shared a room with me and cared for me well in the accommodation and on the train. Perhaps he asked her to join us on the trip to take care of me, showing his concern for me. We can see his attentive personality.

On September 19th 2012, I had a lengthy interview with Didik. The topics were the tradition of transgender plays in Indonesia, his original works, his experiences in Japan, the secret of controlling and manipulating his body, etc. He talked about the various topics for an hour and a half. He answered my questions in detail, also indicating his own thoughts and opinions. His method of speaking fluently to the camera reminded us of the clarity of his thinking as well as his talent as an actor. When I asked a question about the identity of a Chinese Indonesian, he became lost for words and then shed

© Hitoshi Furuya, Gudo, East Java, 2011: Performing a lion dance

tears while discussing the hard experiences of his boyhood. At that time I was moved to see the emotions of an artist who had overcome many hard experiences.

After this, both the photographer and I visited Yogyakarta separately on several more occasions. In January 2013, we met together again when Didik came to Japan for the performance of the "Nanyo Kagura" Project and we could watch his practice, rehearsal, and the show. This book is written based on my observations and impressions of meeting and discussing with him, and watching his performances.

Artistic activities in music and dance are sometimes an artist's means of expressing his identity. In the case of collective performances, the artists aim to achieve the expression of a collective identity. Didik also participates in collaborative works and large-scale artistic events. However, what I was most impressed by after seeing his artistic activity is that he attempts to break through a variety of the boundaries by himself. He always depends on his own body and always tries to answer his own questions in regard to creating something with his body.

He constantly searches for new ideas, and using his great skill, accomplishes what no one else can accomplish. The secret behind the beauty of Didik's performances might be in the challenges he faces in solitude.

© Hitoshi Furuya, Gudo, East Java, 2011: Taking pictures with fans

Afterword: HITOSHI FURUYA

In 2009, I had an offer from Fukuoka-san of Osaka University to make a photo book about Didik Nini Thowok. Although I answered "yes" at that time, I had to carefully consider my approach for documenting this multi-talented artist.

I first met Didik in the latter half of the 1990s. A musician-friend of mine introduced him to me. At that time Indonesia was in the midst of its historical change towards *Reformasi* (reformation), which was followed by the resignation of Suharto in 1998. On this occasion, I had a chance to see the drama play entitled *Hamlet* in Yogyakarta. It was my first time to see Didik perform. He played the role of Hamlet's mother. In the theater I could feel the heated atmosphere. The charged atmosphere may have been because the play was not only about *Hamlet* as a story about a royal family, but was also a metaphorical story that could be overlapped with the political situation at the time. The audience could understand the metaphorical roles of the cast in that play. Didik's performance was well received by the audience, although his role was not the main role in that play as he played the role of the mother through female-impersonation. Later, I had the chance to have a short meeting with Didik. Several months later, Didik came to Japan for a performance after receiving an invitation from the Indonesian embassy in Tokyo. This was

© HITOSHI FURUYA, Yogyakarta, 2013:
Exchanging greetings for Chinese New Year

the first time for me to see his creative work *Dwimuka*. The explanation of this work is in the text of this book. His dancing and movements were so smooth so that I could not differentiate his front from his back. In my long experience of seeing Indonesian dancing since the 1980s, this performance stood out as something new and unique. From then, my friendship with Didik began. I visit him every time I go to Indonesia and Didik also comes to see me every time he travels to Japan.

In the winter of 1999, he planned to stay in Japan and study Japanese dances. Until then Didik had only studied various kinds of dances in different regions of Indonesia. This was not an easy task, even in Indonesia. How much more difficult it would be for him to study Japanese dances in only six months. Many of his friends and teachers were also concerned about this. However, his passion and seriousness alleviated our worries. After learning for six months, Didik held a performance event and played *Hagoromo* and *Fujimusume*. People who have seen Didik are fascinated by his talents as an entertainer as well as by his personality. When we can see passion for arts in a man with such a refined and elegant manner, we become encaptured by him. Didik has wide popularity. In his local area, old women call out to him and shake his hand. In the city, many rickshaw drivers talk to him. Many fans take pictures with him with cameras or cellphones. He, as a friendly artist, always responds to them. People think of him as a member of their family. His popularity arose from his

© HITOSHI FURUYA: Didik's younger sisters

© Hitoshi Furuya, 2013: A photograph with family members

© Hitoshi Furuya, 2013: Staff members in the studio

early performances as a comedian. However, he desires to be regarded as a dancer of traditional, serious dancing and now this conception of him can be seen in Indonesia. Also, he recently works not only as a dancer and performer, but also as a director and a choreographer.

Can I capture his multiple characteristics in my photographs? As discussions about this publication progressed, I hesitated. Existing pictures of him did not accurately portray these and I thought that I would need to have a personal photograph session with him. In January 2013, I joined him on his way back to Indonesia from Japan, and we had several shooting sessions in Yogyakarta. The season coincided with the Chinese New Year or *imlek*, and I got to see another side of Didik, as the head of a big family.

The shootings were conducted in Didik's studio, at some historical sites near Yogyakarta, and at a praying space in the Palace of Yogyakarta. It was the rainy season, so sometimes our shootings were interrupted by the rain. However, this allowed us to shoot pictures with the beautiful sky just after rainfall as the background. In the shooting I endeavored to capture Didik's special charm. Many staff members from Didik's studio supported me, from location hunting to acting as shooting assistants. Thanks to their support, I could capture Didik as I had hoped to and complete the shooting satisfactorily. This shooting was an exciting and important experience for me. I would like to express my gratitude to Didik, who accepted my demands despite his busy schedule, and also to his studio staff who assisted me with my shooting.

Appendix DVD

Appendix DVD

The DVD consists of three parts:
1 Dance Works of DIDIK NINI THOWOK (53 minutes)
2 Street Walk Yogyakarta (4 minutes)
3 DIDIK NINI THOWOK Interview
   by MADOKA FUKUOKA (43 minutes)
   (Translation by MARJORIE SUANDA)

· Providers of film materials:
  Office Moon: *Gambyong Pangkur, Golek Lambangsari,
     Beskalan Putri*
  Didik Nini Thowok Entertainment: *Legong Bapang Saba,
     Nini Thowok, Pancamuka, Panca Sari, Dewi Sarak Jodag, Centhini,
     Bedhaya Hagoromo.*
  HITOSHI FURUYA: Street Walk Yogyakarta,
     DIDIK NINI THOWOK Interview
· Editor of video: HITOSHI FURUYA
  Recording right:
     2013 by Didik Nini Thowok Entertainment,
     MADOKA FUKUOKA & HITOSHI FURUYA
     —

All video materials are recorded using the NTSC system. This video can not be played on other systems such as PAL. All video materials are copyrighted works. Making copies, lending to other people, distributing on the internet, screening, broadcasting, and modification are prohibited. Any infringement of this copyright will be punished according to both criminal and civil law.

Insert the disc to playing device. Choose an option from the 3 options on the menu and press "play" to see it.
Without selecting the option, the video will play in this order: 1 Dance Works, 2 Street Walk, 3 Interview. If the "play" button is not used within 20 seconds, the video will automatically play in the same order.
   For the 1 Dance Works, choose from the sub menu. If the "play" button is not operated within 20 seconds, the video will return to the main menu.
   Even during playing, you can go back to the main menu by operating menu buttons.

DVD CONTENTS 1

Dance Works of DIDIK NINI THOWOK
Performances of original works and classical dances

Original works

- *Dwimuka*: A two faces dance. Didik created this work in the 1980s and since then he has created seven works entitled *Dwimuka*. He has also made a documentary film about the history of the work. Therefore, this work is the most important one for Didik. In *Dwimuka Jepindo*, a characteristic is the wearing of a Japanese mask in front and a Javanese mask on the back of his head. He especially calls the works where five faces including some masks appear as *Pancamuka*. He also has a work entitled *Dwimuka Jali*, where the dancer wears Javanese and Balinese masks.
- *Panca Sari*: A five-elements dance. In this work, Chinese, Indian, Western, Javanese, and Balinese comical elements are expressed. There are many comical plays in this work, so it is popular in Indonesia.
- *Dewi Sarak Jodag*: Based on a Panji Romance from East Java. The title character, Dewi Sarak Jodag, loves Prince Panji Asmarabangun. She disguises her ogre appearance and transforms herself into Panji's lover, Sekartaji. After her disguise is removed, her embarrassment transforms her into an angry woman. This work depicts the various elements of women.
- *Bedhaya Hagoromo*: Based on Japanese old tale "Hagoromo" in which a heavenly maiden performs her dancing for a fisherman for taking back her robe of feathers. This work is a collaborative work based on both a Japanese *noh* play and a Javanese court dance, *bedhaya*, in which nine female dancers appear.

Classical dances

- *Gambyong Pangkur*: Traditional Javanese female dance. This dance derived from the welcome dance. *Pangkur* is the name of the tune.
- *Golek Lambangsari*: One of the classical dance styles in Yogyakarta. This dance features the young girl's gestures of making up and grooming. *Lambangsari* is the name of the tune.
- *Beskalan Putri*: A female dance from East Java, depicting the appearance of general femininity.
- *Legong Bapan Saba*: A Balinese traditional female dance originating from the Saba region.

DVD CONTENTS 2

Street Walk Yogyakarta

Street Walk Yogyakarta (railway station, post office, bank, palace, market, Malioboro street), Didik's former office and studio (moved to new location in 2016)

Interview by MADOKA FUKUOKA
(Translation by MARJORIE SUANDA)

Q What is the difference between female artists playing female roles and male artists playing female roles?

A According to my observations, for a woman to dance the character of a woman is easier, because it is already part of her nature, so it is not necessary to study special techniques. But if a man is to play a woman or perform as an *onnagata*, that requires extra practice because, from the posture of his body and so forth, he is a man. So, when he expresses the character of a woman, he has to observe closely, become familiar with, and practice how to execute the movements well and ensure that they are movements that are perfectly suited to the character of the woman he is portraying.

Q How do you include masculinity when playing a woman (*onnagata*)?

A It will be in accordance with the theme or the character. For example, when a woman expresses feelings of anger, the movements that emerge are rather masculine, rough, and in this situation these movements can be used. But there is a difference. The strong movements of a man and the strong movements of a woman will still be different. However, if it is an *onnagata* dancer with a lot of experience, who has been practicing for years and understands how to express a woman's dance well, one who is already professional, he will not have a problem because he understands what the right amount is when he must express the masculinity of a woman.

Q What elements of masculinity are in the work *Dewi Sarak Jodag*?

A In the last part of *Dewi Sarak Jodag*, I express the characer of a female ogre, or

the role suggested by the expression on the mask, but the idea or power is that of a woman playing a strong, rough character. This is a feeling I applied when I studied *topeng* Cirebon (the masked dances of Cirebon), because most of my teachers of *topeng* Cirebon were women who played the characters of men. For example, my teachers were the late Ibu Suji, Ibu Rasinah, and Ibu Sawitri. They were all women who could play male characters extraordinarily well, but they were still women playing men, not men playing men. Because I am an *onnagata* artist, my power is perhaps different from that of a masculine man. My masculinity when playing a strong character is that of a woman playing a strong male.

Q What are the conditions of the daily lives of transgender (cross-gender) performers of traditional arts?

A As far as I know, there are two kinds of cross-gender or transgender individuals. There are those who in everyday life are transgender individuals whose appearance is like a woman, their image is always that of a woman. In these modern times there are some who will undergo operations, they will have their breasts enlarged or even have their genitals altered. But there is also a group of cross-gender people for whom such practices do not enter their everyday lives, so they do not dress as women in daily life. There are even some cross-gender individuals who marry women and father children.

Q What is the response of society towards transgender (cross-gender) performers?

A In the past, when the tradition of cross-gender still flourished in society, people could accept it and it was not something strange, especially in areas where the tradition of cross-gender existed and developed, as well as in areas where there were cross-gender art forms, as in Surabaya where there is *ludruk*, as in Malang and Jombang, or in Sulawesi where there is the tradition of the *bissu* priests.

Indeed, these times are very different from in the past, particularly in the performing arts since women started to take part in performances on stage. According to a book written by professor Soedarsono, who wrote about the history of this tradition, women began to appear on stage in the 20th century. One of the things that happened in the Yogyakarta court in the past, before the 20th century, was that women's roles in *wayang wong* were played by males, and young boys were chosen who were about 13 to 15 years old. Physically, their bodies were still slim, they were not yet muscular, and their Adam's apples had not yet developed. They would choose those who had beautiful or handsome faces so when they were made up as women you could not tell if they were actually men or women.

Q What is the difference between transgender performers in traditional arts and *waria* or *banci* (transvestites)?

A They are actually different. *Banci*, especially nowadays, have a tendency towards prostitution in their everyday lives. Not all, but usually they wear makeup and sell themselves at night. The image of *banci* or *waria* in society is that of someone who is involved in prostitution. But, in Makassar there are two groups of *waria*. One group called *calabai* indeed sell themselves and the others are priests or what are often called *bissu*. So they are very different. And in the performing arts there are cross-gender people who may be *banci*, but they do not prostitute themselves

because they already have a position or profession in society, such as that of a stage artist. And there are also those who have the profession of beauticians, they work in or own beauty salons, and so forth. The same as in society, it is a personal choice; there are *waria* or *banci* who choose to prostitute themselves or those who look for a profession that is respected in society.

But, in my observations or according to my information, the reason a cross-gender persons would sell themselves is because initially they were not accepted in society or perhaps they were not even accepted in their family. Perhaps they were ostracized or marginalized, so their skills or expertise did not develop, maybe because in school they did not get a good education, they were members of a minority, they did not get sufficient attention from their teachers, or they were ashamed and isolated themselves. So the only way, or one of the easiest ways, for them to make money is to prostitute themselves.

But honestly, if they were asked if they want to do that, they would not prostitute themselves, but they are stuck, *kepepet*, or trapped, in the sense that there is no other way they could develop a profession, and they could not get a good education, so then finally they resort to prostitution.

Q What is your opinion of the Anti Pornography and Porno Action Bill?

A Actually the pornography bill, if it is used within the correct limits of that which is categorized as porno, I agree with it. But, if it involves performing arts, in which for example, Javanese dancers, *Gambyong* dancers, since long ago wore costumes called *kemben* (ed., *batik* material wrapped over the breasts and torso, with the shoulders left bare). Then if that is categorized as a form of pornography, I do not agree and I am, indeed, really opposed to that. I took part in a demonstration against that

139

pornography law. So they can apply the pornography law, but they have to look first. That which is called pornography, what are the limits? It cannot be made all the same, for example, if the shoulders are left bare it is categorized as porno, but what about if it involves the arts?

Moreover, in the *kraton* or palace, as traditional clothing for weddings or what is called *besanan*, from the past until today, they have worn *kemben*, which are also with bare shoulders. So lawmakers must be very wise in applying this rule and in categorizing that which is porno and that which is traditional. We cannot apply the same standards to these two categories. People who wore those traditional clothes in the past were not trying to exploit sexiness or porno, but because it is a part of their traditional customs.

If we go back to the past, like in Bali, in the past, people, when they danced or in everyday life, only covered themselves from the waist down, so women's upper bodies were naked. It was not a problem then, so why is it a problem now? Perhaps, because we have regulations. And it doesn't mean that people who dress like that are uncivilized. We must be very careful when we say that something is civilized or uncivilized. Maybe people who are fully dressed are more uncivilized than people who are partly naked.

There are men in Papua who only wear a *koteka* (penis gourd) and are bare at the top, but we can't say that they are more uncivilized than modern people who wear a full suit, with a tie and a handsome jacket. Maybe people who dress traditionally in Papua are more civilized, and many of those who know modern ways are more uncivilized.

Q What is your opinion of the rights of sexual minorities?

A Nowadays, with human rights, many kinds of laws, developments over time, and influences from outside, communities such as those of gays and lesbians have been established. If we talk about human rights, and if we want to become a developed country, we have to take examples from other countries: That these groups exist.

And, if we want to be honest, if we talk about homosexuality, from the past it existed, but in the past it was not too exposed and their behavior was not too "over-acting". What then made people in society antipathetic towards them was when they began over-acting. So then, they stood out too much and it was that over-acting which made people dislike them.

Q What is required to construct the body of a cross-gender dancer (*onnagata*)?

A Yes, one thing that is important, that we have to be aware of, for example, like for me as an artist or a stage performer, we have to take care of our appearance. For example, how we care for our face with what products and also the physical proportions of our body are very important.

One simple example: For people who are 50 years old or older, the thing that grows the fastest is the stomach. I have also experienced this. So, we have to think about how to take care so our stomach doesn't grow too much because, if it grows too large, it is not beautiful, especially if we have to perform as a beautiful woman.

It's also a problem for costumes. If the costumes we wore when we were still thin do not fit anymore and we have to

make new ones, that's a problem. But that can be avoided by paying attention to the food we eat.

For the face, we have to think about the way we care for it. I have reduced my use of beauty-care products that are too chemical-based. I use natural materials and not too many chemical-based products.

For example, there is a natural whitening powder I found in India. Actually there are many traditional ingredients, if we want to be diligent in looking for them. Indeed, the traditional ones are not too popular, but they are more original and have fewer side effects. I found this whitening powder in India and the material was made from a kind of stone.

If I am not mistaken, in the past in China there was a material for makeup, something called *atalwatu*. It was hard like a stone, like limestone, but could be softened, mixed with water, and could be used as powder.

Q Do you use traditional Javanese makeup?

A In Java there is something called *wedak adem* or a cool powder. It is made from rice flour mixed with, I don't know what, then made into powder that in the past was worn by elderly women at night. It was really good, because it made the skin soft, but it is rarely used now. I also rarely use it, but sometimes I do use it. When I performed *Centhini*, I remembered this cool powder, and I used it as face powder to express *Centhini* at night, because the figure of *Centhini* here is without a prominent character, so I made her white, like using the whitening powder.

Q What is the secret of controlling the shape of the body?

A It is actually not a secret, because I want to share it here. We have to consume a lot of fruit and vegetables and reduce the amount of rice we eat. Because in Indonesia rice as the carbohydrate is our staple food, but it is what makes the stomach grow. We also must reduce the amount of oil we eat. Secondly, if we are interested in yoga, it is very helpful

to practice breathing. My yoga teacher is from India and taught me about breathing into the stomach and that is what I often practice. It is not just for health, but yoga is also for breathing, because for a dancer, breath is also very important, breath is life.

Q How did you design the choreography for *Panca Sari*?

A Like one of the examples that I demonstrated yesterday, the dance is titled *Panca Sari* or five elements, *panca* means five, *sari* means elements. In it I want to show that in the dances of Indonesia there is much influence from Chinese culture. In the dances of Bali, Cirebon, Betawi, Bayuwangi, and in many other places the influence of Chinese culture is very strong. Then, in *Panca Sari* there is also Western influence, as in the dance that uses hiphop music and features robotic movements. This shows that in Indonesia there are also modern influences. And then I still include traditional influences, comedy and, lastly, with *dangdut* music, the influence from India is very strong. With the emergence of *dangdut* music and many Indian songs translated into Indonesian, the influence from India is strong. These are the five elements that I show and we can clearly see their influences in society at large.

Q How do you express your identity as a Chinese-Indonesian?

A For me that is very complicated. Because, from the time I was a child, my grandfather took me to see Javanese performing arts, so Javanese arts are a part of me. Javanese arts are just a natural part of my life. Now, in today's era, when Chinese culture has been allowed to emerge, in my opinion, it's good, because people can express themselves more, especially those who are of Chinese descent. But I also still remember some of the events that have taken place in the past in Indonesia, for example, the events of 1965, and when the Chi-

nese had to change their names.

I experienced it in 1965, I was 11 (eleven) years old in 1965, so I was in grade 5 or 6 of elementary school and I can still remember clearly feeling the fear and the tension.

Moreover, when I was in junior high school my grandfather had already thought about it and decided that I should go to a public or state school, rather than the Christian school, which was predominantly Chinese. So when I entered SMP Negeri I (State Junior High School No.1), I was the one and only student of Chinese descent with a Chinese name. I still clearly remember having stones thrown at me, being called names, "Cina, Cina" and being beaten up. I really experienced the fear and........ So, I experienced that, and I became very introverted. I was fearful, shy, scared to appear in public. But with my profession in dance, it helped me, because it gave me self-confidence. I had the courage to appear in public. It made me able to change from an introvert to an extrovert and, especially by becoming involved in comedy, that changed my style in life and my personality.

Sometimes the introverted side of me emerges if I am not performing, when I appear in public I sometimes become shy and groggy. If I am in a forum and have to speak, I feel like, "Eeh, how can I do this?"

But if I am in a dance costume on stage I can change, I become someone else. In my process in the arts I have to be able to take control over the stage, I have to become the king of the stage. I never look at who is in the audience. Basically, I enter into the character and I forget everything around me when I am dancing, so that is what made me able to change.

So, performing in public can help to change a person's personality and that is my own experience.

Q Would you like to do your artistic activity as a Chinese-Indonesian artist?

A It's okay, sometimes I'm like that. I also had to speak for TED International. I had to talk about myself, but when I got to that part, I became emotional like this. I'm sorry. I think maybe it is because the memories are still strong. But, I want to continue. So I experienced those years. Until now, I didn't want to express too much that I am Chinese, I am an Indonesian, but I am a descendant of Chinese, there is no denying that.

I was born of a Chinese father and a Javanese mother. That cannot be denied, even though I could lie to people if I wanted to. If I said I'm Javanese, who would not believe me? But I don't want to, because my purpose is to educate the younger generations and I want to be honest to myself.

I want to speak out to people in Indonesia that the stereotypical image Indonesians have of Chinese people as only identical with business, commercial endeavors, economy, and money is not completely true. Many Chinese people have played an important role in the preservation of culture in Java, Bali, Sunda, and in many other areas, but during the Suharto era they were afraid to expose themselves or to appear too prominently.

But today, when many people know my biography and know that I am of Chinese descent, many in the Chinese community are proud that they have me, someone who is Chinese and has excelled in the Javanese arts. But I myself, I say I am an Indonesian. And I will show in the eyes of the world that I am an Indonesian and I want to make my country well known, so although I'm of Chinese descent, I can do a lot for Indonesia.

Q What do you think about the activity of being a comedian?

A Actually, if I can talk about this, it is something I've discussed with other artists.

Comedy is actually higher, or at a different level, than serious art. A comedian can undertake the serious, but it is not necessarily true that a serious artist can perform comedy. I experienced this also in dance. I became a comic dancer, but I went through studying dances seriously, traditional dances. When I studied Javanese dance, Balinese dance, and dances from other places, at first I learned serious dances. Once I had well and truly mastered the technique of the serious dances, then I could perform them more towards comedy, because I knew the rules, so they were easier to play with.

Perhaps, it is like someone in the legal world, sometimes they play with the law. If they are someone who already has mastered law, they can play around with the laws and trick people because they are already an expert in the laws. So for me, it is just the same, because if I play with comedy it is because I have already mastered the fixed tradition, the main rules.

But, in the performing arts in Indonesia, people already know me as a comedian and I am more popular as a comedy dancer, so that people expect me to perform as a dancer and act funny. People will not like it if I perform without being funny. That is one of the problems in Indonesia, because I once tried it. It doesn't mean that I cannot dance serious dances, those are the basics of my background, but I once tried to perform without being funny. I performed serious dances and many people in the audience complained. "Mas Didik, why weren't you funny? I was waiting for the funny parts. I came here and paid a lot of money for tickets because I want to see you perform comedy, not dance serious dances".

So sometimes that's the problem, yes, here we have to look at the market, too. When I began to combine the worlds of business and the performing arts, one of the important aspects is that we have to examine the market. While in other countries it is very different because, indeed, in other countries they often view all Indonesian dances as serious; moreover, those who appear abroad rarely perform comic dancing. Even in Indonesia my group and I are the only pioneers of comic dance who still exist today. So, it's the same.

When I first began to perform abroad, one experience that was very interesting for me was when I performed in Japan. I danced a comic dance and at first the audience did not understand. Maybe they thought it was funny, and they wanted to laugh but they held it in. Usually they had seen Indonesian performances that are serious, there were none that were comedies, so when they wanted to laugh, they held it in. I clearly remember once when I performed in Osaka or Tokyo, after the performance was over there was a woman in the audience who came backstage and she asked for forgiveness. She laughed and laughed until she cried, because when she was watching she wasn't brave enough to laugh so she held it until she met me backstage, then she laughed until she cried. I was impressed by that and it was funny. So, in several countries there is an announcement at the beginning, "If you want to laugh, please feel free to do so, if you want to clap, please do, because this is a comic performance". This is because the rules in other countries are that applause must be held until the end of the performance. But in Indonesia, if I perform and they like it, they spontaneously applaud and sometimes shout. That's common here. So, the first time I was in America and saw the audience was so quiet, I was shocked. Oh, no one was responding. It turns out that the culture is different. But after I have visited a country a number of times, and I have an audience that is familiar with me, they begin to understand. "Oh, so if we watch a performance of Mas Didik dancing, we are free to laugh and applaud. When you watch comedy, to laugh as loud as you like is okay". So that's one of the

differences if I dance in Idonesia and abroad.

Q How important is your experience of studying cross-gender or *onnagata* in other countries?

A Yes, that was a very valuable experience for me. Because when I studied *onnagata* in Japan, it turned out *onnagata* as an artist or as a branch of the performing arts is highly valued by the public. This is also true in China, Chinese Opera, and also in India. Whereas in Indonesia because I pioneered *onnagata* art, I experienced a rather difficult process. So, from the time I introduced it until today, it is only now that people are beginning to understand it. In the beginning it was very difficult indeed. And there is a difference, because when I met with *onnagata* artists from Japan, from China, from India, they asked me, "Why do you perform a female character and make it into a joke, so it becomes comedy, while in Japan or in China, it is very serious?" An *onnagata* artist performs a female character who is perfect; there is no joking at all. So for me that was something new to learn and very interesting. Then, I thought about it, and I could answer, because the situation of the people in Indonesia is very different. After I observed and analyzed it, they accept me as a comedian, even though at times I long to dance as an *onnagata* and perform a serious dance, which I can only present when I perform abroad. If I dance a *golek* dance or Balinese dance without joking, I can only do so when I perform abroad, because in Indonesia it is difficult. In my observations, for the public in Indonesia, which is still a developing country, daily life is so full of a high level of stress, because of the economy and because life is not settled, not yet well established, and so they laugh easily. They need something that can make them laugh to release or decrease their stress. Thus, if I perform a comic dance, they can immediately laugh heartily and that helps them. It is a kind of healing for them, so that it releases them from the stress they experience in their daily lives. Thus, in Indonesia, comedy is very welcomed, easily accepted on television programs and such.... that was one of the beginnings.

Nonetheless, at one time, there was a ban by the government on male performers playing women on TV. There were exceptions. I had already begun to demonstrate that men performing as women is actually a serious art form. Even though I had to do so with comedy, the way I performed it was still serious, in the sense that I designed the costume seriously, the dance movements were also not just fooling around, and if I wanted to perform comedy it was all done with choreography that was neatly arranged.

Q Tell us about your social activities as an artist.

A Actually, my social activities are based on the belief system I follow. I am a Christian, a Protestant, and in our teachings we learn that we must donate that which we have received. Even according to the teachings of the Bible, we must give one-tenth to the church. Each month we do not only give to the church, but donate to poor people, orphans, or others who are in need. The basis is just that. So, also in the arts, because my talent is as a dancer, I try to fulfill those teachings. I do that in accordance with my religion, the basis is just that. And from the past, if I get some good fortune, I donate it to others. This was instilled in me since I was small, when I went to Sunday school at church, and also through the philosophy of my own family. My grandfather, who was Chinese, and my mother, who was Javanese, they did that. If we can we should give to others, not just ask for things, but whatever amount we can give, our intention to give is already something valuable. So, if we give, we do so wholeheartedly and willingly, and we don't expect anything in return. Those were the teachings instilled in us in our family as well as at church. And maybe because from the time I was child that was always taught to me, I always heard that, so in my life today I apply that. And if we want to be honest, if we really follow that, our lives will be good and what is called good fortune will continue to flow. It's like if we have a container, if we always throw out some of the contents, there will always be an empty place. So if something else wants to come into the container, there is space for it. But if the container is already full and we don't take anything out, then there is no place to put anything else. I don't know if this is true or not, because I'm not clever in philosophy....hehe (laugh)..... I only follow it.

Q What are your plans for the next generation?

A There are actually many of my friends who ask me, "Do you already have the next generation who can follow you to continue your work? Not yet?" I ask, "Which followers?" Indeed, I have a lot of students in my dance school. But I differentiate, the dances that I teach to my students and the dances I use for performing, they are different. So here I apply management in the sense that I follow the techniques of management in other fields. I've observed, for example, restaurants; there is the Ayam Goreng Suharti (Suharti's Chicken) restaurant chain in Indonesia. The spices for Suharti's Chicken are not taught to other people. It is the secret of Ayam Suharti. So that is the approach I use. I think there are many other restaurants that also have secret recipes. So simply, I learned that from restaurants. I thought, "I can do that too". I can keep as a secret or monopolize the arts or dances that I perform, so what I teach are other dances. Then there is not a lot of competition in the market. That is the approach I follow.

If I am asked about the next generation, sometimes I think of my students who could carry on my specific dances, like the two-faced dance. But to find students like that is not easy, because we have to equip them with many dances that have different ethnic backgrounds or different types of dances that they can perform well. And I was like that, I studied Javanese dance in Yogya and Solo styles, Sundanese dances, Sumatran dances, Balinese dances, and so on. I really studied them seriously, well and truly, and I was consistent in always doing female dances. Because there are many dancers who are able to dance female dances but are not consistent, they also dance male dances. It's not that that is not allowed, you certainly can do that, but for me, if I am going to seriously study as an *onnagata* artist, I am going to concentrate and be consistent as an *onnagata* or cross-gender performer. And that will be different.

If there is a student who is also like that and is interested, I will also be happy to teach him. Because to pass on my knowledge, it is not enough to simply find a student who is talented, but there are many aspects or considerations. It's clear, number one, the student should have talent. That is certain. Secondly, he must have a good character, not be dishonest or unethical, because sometimes we see artists who forget history. What I mean is, they do not value the teachers who gave them something, or people who provided some service to this artist. That is something I don't agree with.

Sometimes I demonstrate or give an example. For example, I studied Cirebon masked dances in 1979 in Palimanan and I maintain respect for my teacher. I just got back from Cirebon one month or two months ago, where I visited the grave of my late teacher. It is something I always do, and I always communicate with the family of my late teacher. And in Bali, I do the same. And in Malang..... I just returned from

Malang, where I went to dance and, coincidentally, the stage was in front of my late teacher's home. So an example I always give to the younger generation is to value and respect people who have done you a service, because I believe in karma. If we plant something in a good way, then we also reap what is good. But if we plant in a way that isn't right, just wait and see.... It will be proven, is it true or not? True or not....

Q What is your source of energy as a dancer?

A The question is interesting, but difficult to answer. The source of energy actually, if we feel that we already have the profession of a dancer, it must be done with a sincere heart and with love. When we love our profession, when we are devoted and work hard at our profession, we have to do it totally: With all of our life, heart and soul, with a high level of totality. And one of the points is, that as human beings, never stop learning. I always apply this. I never feel satisfied, or never feel that I am already clever enough. No. I still must always learn, because for me, life is learning.

In any country, when I arrive there and I meet other artists, I feel like, well, it turns out, I cannot do this dance, I don't know this art form. The more I see and the more I meet artists from other countries, the more it makes me realize, I'm nothing yet. Maybe other people view me and think, "Wow, Mas Didik is already a master of this or that, of A, B, C", or that I am already extraordinary, but I myself feel like, oh, not yet. Because if I visit some other region, for example, in Japan, I've only studied a tiny bit about *Nihon buyo* and *noh* drama, but there are so many other art forms in Japan. There are Okinawan dances, there is *kagura* and many, many others that I don't yet know. So I've only studied a little, but other Indonesians look at me and think, "Wow, Mas Didik has already mastered all these Japanese dances". Actually, in

my heart of hearts I am embarrassed, but here because they themselves have not studied, they think that I am extraordinary. But I feel like I haven't done anything yet. If I'm in Japan and see *taishuengeki* (popular theater), or see Takarazuka, *Nihon buyo*, or *kabuki*, I'm just amazed, because I look at them with sincerity.

There is one thing that we have to remember, if we want to succeed, we have to have the concept of empty, zero or emptiness. So we don't position ourselves as anything. Like when I went to Japan to study *Nihon buyo*, I emptied myself, I'm nothing, I'm just Didik, period. I'm not an artist, even though at the time I was already a well-known artist in Indonesia. But in Japan, no one knew me, who was I? I had to be able to just be myself, I am an Indonesian who wants to study Japanese dance. That is what saves me in any place, so that I can be accepted. Be sincere and honest and live simply, because I've seen many friends who are too "*jaim*" (*jaga image*) or are trying to protect their image, pretending; As if because they are artists, if they go anywhere they have to go by taxi or they have to take a limousine, for example. But for me, if I go by *becak* (rickshaw), it's okay, if I walk it's no problem, because I don't want to be burdened by all those kinds of attributes. If I'm burdened by all of that, it's hard to live. I want to live lightly, easily. So if I go anywhere, I just bring myself like this, it's easy. I don't want to be burdened by any of that stuff. I still want to eat at roadside stalls just like everybody. Indeed, I come from an ordinary background. Becoming famous is just an opportunity given to us by God, so I can go abroad dozens of times, or get this and that. Other people can evaluate it, but what's important is that I'm just like this....Crazy....haha (laugh), I am indeed crazy.

All done? You are welcome....

Bibliography

Aoki, Yoko
2006 Indonesia kakyo-kajin kenkyushi: Suharto jidai kara kaikaku no jidai eno tenkan, *Tonan Asia Kenkyu* 43 (4): 397–418 (The history of research on Indonesian-Chinese: Changes since the era of the Suharto order to the era of reformation)

Boellstorff, Tom
2003 Dubbing culture: Indonesian gay and lesbi subjectivities and ethnography in an already globalized world, *American Ethnologsist* 30, pp. 225–242.

Fukuoka, Madoka
2010 Transmission of skills: A case study of the Cirebonese masked dance. *Bulletin of the Graduate School of Human Sciences* (Osaka University) vol. 36: 243–262.
2014 Cross-gender attempts by Indonesian female-impersonator dancer Didik Nini Thowok. *Wacana Seni Journal of Arts Discourse*. Vol. 13: 57–83.
2015 A study of femininity and masculinity: Gender and sexuality in Indonesian popular culture. *Osaka Human Sciences*. Vol. 1: 95–115.

Heryanto, Ariel
2014 *Identity and Pleasure: The Politics of Indonesian Screen Culture*. (KYOTO CSEAS SERIES ON ASIAN STUDIES 13, Center for Southeast Asian Studies, Kyoto University), NUS Press Singapore in association with Kyoto University Press.

Hughes-Freeland, Felicia
2008 Cross-dressing across cultures: Genre and gender in the dances of Didik Nini Thowok. *ARI Working Paper* No. 108. November 2008, https://ari.nus.edu.sg/Publication/Detail/1264. pp. 3–37.
2010 Creativity and cross-cultural collaboration: The case of Didik Nini Thowok's *BEDHAYA HAGOROMO*. In L. Nozlopy and M. Cohen (eds.) *Contemporary Southeast Asian performance: Transnational perspectives*. Newcastle: Cambridge Scholars, pp. 25–45.
2012 Japanese-Indonesian hybridity? The case of Didik Nini Thowok's Bedhaya Hagoromo. In Mohd Anis Md Nor (eds.) *Dancing mosaic: Issues on dance hybridity*, Kuala Lumpur: Cultural Center University of Malaya and National Department for Culture and Arts Ministry of Information Communication and Culture Malaysia.

Janarto, Henry Gendut
2005 *Didik Nini Thowok: Menari sampai lahir kembali*. Malang: Sava Media

Kazama, Junko
1994 *Jawa no otofukei*. Tokyo: Mecong (Soundscape in Java)

Lindsay, Jennifer
2011 Media and morality: Pornography post Suharto. In Krishna Sen and David T. Hill (eds.) *Politics and the Media in Twenty-First Century Indonesia*. London and New York: Routledge, pp. 172–195.

Melamed, E.
1983 *Mirror, mirror: The terror of not being young*. New York: Linden Press/Simon & Schuster.

Mrázek, Jan
2005 Masks and selves in comtemporary Java: The dances of Didik Nini Thowok. *Journal of Southeast Asian Studies*, 36 (2), pp. 249–279.

Oetomo, Dede
1996 Gender and sexual orientation in Indonesia. In Laurie J. Sears (ed.) *Fantasizing the feminine in Indonesia*. Durham: Duke University Press, pp. 259–269.

Peacock, James
1987 *Rites of modernization: Symbols and social aspects of Indonesian proletarian drama* (with a new afterword). Chicago: The University of Chicago Press. (first edition in 1968.)

Sutton, R. Anderson
1991 *Traditions of gamelan music in Java: Musical pluralism and regional identity*. Cambridge: Cambridge University Press.

Tsuda, Koji
2010 Ima, Jawa no jibyou de nani ga okotte iruka: Post Suharto ki Indonesia no Kokka, shukyo, kajin komyunity, *Asia Africa gengo bunka kenkyu* 79: 37–71. (What is happening in the Chinese temple in Java: Nation, religion, Chinese community)
2011 *Kajinsei no minzokushi: Taisei tenkan ki Indonesia no field kara*. Kyoto: Sekaishisosha. (Ethnography of Chineseness: From the field in changing regime Indonesia.)

Index   * Numbers with asterisk denote
                                            reference to pictures.

Aa
APPAN (Asia Pacific Performing
   Arts Network) 101,104
assimilation 019,054,056
ASTI (Akademi Seni Tari Indonesia) 022
Ardhanareesvara 004–005*,112–113*,
   114

Bb
Bagong Kussudiardjo 022
banci 025,065,139
Banyumas 024,110,114
bedhaya 024,066
Bedhaya Hagoromo 029,066,093*,
   120*,121,122–123*
Beskalan Putri 032,036–038*
bun 043,045,088–090

Cc
Chinatown 056,081,083
Chinese Indonesian 019,052–053,
   056–057,074,143–144
Chineseness 053,057,061
Chinese Temple 075–076,077*,
   080*,081
Cirebon 043,046,068,092,147
comedian 062,064,066,144
costume 026–027,030,032,
   042–044,078,090–091,141
cross-gender 025,065,067,069,104,
   121,138–139,141,146–147

Dd
dalang 046
dalang topeng 046
dangdut 058,143
Dewi Sarak Jodag 068–069,
   070–072*,089,092*,094,138
Dewi Sri 110
Dwimuka 040*,041–042
Dwimuka IMB 156–157*
Dwimuka Jali 048–049*
Dwimuka Jepindo 042–045

Ee
essentialism 061
ethnic 019,056
ethnicity 019–020,044

Ff
female-impersonating dancer 028–029,
   055,066
female impersonation 020,024,029,
   046
female-role 024–025,069,101
femininity 020,027,040,044,069
Fujian 052

Gg
gagah 046,092
gamelan 018
Gambyong Pangkur 030–031,032*
gender 019–020,044,065,069,091
Golek Lambangsari 018*,029–030
Gudo 075–076,077*,080*

Hh
Hong Sang Kiong 075–076,077*

Ii
identity 056–057,061,074,143
Indramayu 046,047*,093
ISI (Institute Seni Indonesia) 022

Jj
jaipongan 031–032,033*,043,110,114
jatilan/kuda kepang 019

Kk
kagura 099,148
kemben 030,139–140
ketoprak 019
Klana topeng 022*
klenteng 056,075
kraton 140
Kushinadahime 110,111*

I52

Ll

Lambangsari (tune) 029
Lambangsari (group) 091
legong 031,042,045,096
Legong Bapan Saba 034-035*
lengger 024,110
linyep 046,092
Losari 046,093
ludruk 024,118,119*,139

Mm

makeup 027,055,078,086-088,142
masculinity 027,069,138
mask 042-046,089-094,100,110
minority 056,139,141

Nn

National Dance Academy (see also ASTI)
    019,025,028,055
Natya Lakshita 019,055,106
Nanyo Kagura 099,100*
ngamen 097
Nini Thowok 054*,055
noh 029,066,067*,068,094,096,
    121,148

Oo

"One Table Two Chairs" (project) 104
onnagata 066-067,101,119-121*,
    138,141,146-147

Pp

Palimanan 046,050*,092,147
Panca Sari 059-060*,062,078,093,
    143
Panji 068-069,072,092,094
Peacock, James 024
pekan budaya Tionghoa Yogyakarta 081
peranakan 056,074

Rr

Ramayana 022,024,027
Rasinah 046,047*,093,138
REBORN 118

Ss

Sawitri 046,093,138
sendratari 018,022
sexual minority 026,141
sinetron 064
Suharto 019
Sonobudoyo museum 022
srimpi 022*
Suharto order 053,056
Suji 046,050*,092-093,096,138
sultan 022,083,118
Sultan Hamengkubuwono X 022,084*,
    123*

Tt

tata rias 055
topknot 078,089*,090
Tumanggung 019,052
topeng Cirebon 046,096,138
transgender 019,024,026,066,121,
    138
transvestite 024-026,139

Uu

UU APP (*Undang-Undang Anti
    Pornografi dan Pornoaksi*) 026,139

Vv

voice 091

Ww

warga keturunan asing 056
watak 046
wayang 018,022
wayang kulit 022,046
wayang potehi 075,080,083*
wayang wong 122*,139
waria 025,065,139
wig 088-090

Yy

yoga 086,142-143
Yogyakarta 018,022,081-083,084*,
    096-097,104,118,121

About the Author
and the Photographer

Author
MADOKA FUKUOKA (Ph. D) is a
professor of the course of Anthropology
at the Graduate School of Human
Sciences, Osaka University in Japan.
    Her research interests include
1) transmission of skills in performing
art forms, 2) gender imagery in
Indonesian dancing and theater,
and 3) identity and popular culture
in Southeast Asia.

Photographer
HITOSHI FURUYA is a photographer
of the stage photographs of dance
performances, the commercial
photographs, and the magazine
photogravures.
    He is a member of Japan Professional
Stage Photographers Society.
    He is active in the getting data of
performing art forms in Asian countries
especially Bali and Java in Indonesia.

Providers of Pictures
• Didik Nini Thowok Entertainment
• Lambangsari (gamelan group in Japan)
• Naoya Ikegami
• Indonesian National TV Station
  The branch office of Yogyakarta

Special Thanks for
Mr. Richard Emert
Mr. Alex Dea
Mr. Tetsuro Koyano
Mr. Kei Wada
Mr. Makoto Sato
Ibu Warjinah
Special thanks for the help of
Sri Sultan Hamengkubuwono X (10th)

▶ The scenes from the
work *Dwimuka Jepindo*,
the most popular work in
the serial works of *Dwimuka*.
It expresses Japanese
(Jepang) and Indonesian
elements.

The scenes from the work entitled *Dwimuka IMB*. Didik puts the mask of old person on his front and the clown mask on his back. The design of the fabrics used for the costume are derived from the motifs of the clouds called *Mega Mendung*. These fabrics are known as *batik* from the Cirebon area, the northwest part in Java.

The scenes from the work entitled *Dewi Sarak Jodag*. Didik, known as the dancer in skillful comical plays, composed this serious work in 2004. The story of the work is derived from the Javanese Panji Romance. Sarak Jodag, who plays the title role, seduces Prince Panji by disguising as the prince's lover, Sekar Taji.

Didik wears the Japanese *Otafuku* mask and a costume inspired by the Japanese kimono on his front, and performs the elegant female Japanese dance. While performing the dynamic Javanese folk dance, he wears the Balinese mask and Javanese costume on his back. (see p.155)